Discipline
What Nobody Wants to Hear
Jermaine Jefferson

GrowFitFL LLC

CONTENTS

For my father.
You never said the word. You just lived it every single day.
I finally understand.
And for my wife, my kids, and every person who goes to bed tonight hyping
a future date instead of living in the present moment.
This one is for you.

WHO THIS BOOK IS FOR

This book is for the person who calls themselves a hard worker and means it, but somehow keeps quitting the things that could actually change their life.

It's for you who have tried motivation. You've watched the videos, read the quotes, downloaded the apps, bought the supplements, and drunk enough caffeine to power a small city. You felt unstoppable for approximately thirty minutes. Then real life showed up, and you were right back where you started.

You're a good person with real ambition. You can picture exactly what you want your life to look like. But every night you go to bed making promises to a future version of yourself - what you're going to do tomorrow, next Monday, next month, when things settle down, when the time is right.

And every morning the action doesn't come. Just more planning. More preparing. More waiting for a perfect moment that never arrives.

I know you because I was you.

This book isn't about motivation. It's about the thing that comes after motivation fails - and it always fails. It's about discipline. Not the kind you perform for other people. The kind you build in private, in the dark, when nobody is watching and nobody will ever know.

That kind of discipline will change everything in your life. From your health to your marriage. Your relationship with your kids. Your finances and your future.

But it starts with telling yourself the truth.

That's what we're going to do in these pages.

Daytona Beach, $400, and the Rest of My Life

I want to tell you about the worst meal I ever had.

The last football team I would ever play for had just cut me. Done. No more tryouts, no more chances, no more telling myself that this time would be different. The dream I had carried since I was a kid was officially over, and I was sitting in my car in a parking lot trying to figure out what that meant.

So I drove. With no other ideas, I simply aimed the car south and drove for sixteen hours without stopping. I'd always heard about Daytona Beach. I figured I'd spend a couple of days on the beach, clear my head, and figure out my next steps. What I hadn't fully accounted for was that I had about $400 to my name, and most of that needed to get me back home.

I was planning to sleep in my car. Eat Little Caesars hot and ready pizza. Five dollars a day, stretch it out, get my mind right.

And then I drove past this restaurant.

I don't know if it was the smell, or the music, or the way Daytona Beach looked that evening, or honestly just one more act of self-sabotage from a man who had gotten very good at it. Whatever it was, I sat down. Ordered the meal you order when you're trying to feel like your life isn't falling apart. Heavy on the drinks. And when the check came - $160 - something in me just shut off.

Not loud tears. Not a breakdown. Just the feeling that enough is enough. I sat there with a $160 check, $400 to my name, no business, no football career, no plan, just thoughts of how good it would feel to not be alive anymore. How somehow, not existing would be the escape that I needed from the living hell that I created.

I felt like a fraud. Not just in that moment, - in my whole life. I had worked hard my entire life. I came out of high school ready to outwork everyone. My father had installed something in me I thought was enough. Work ethic. Grit. Show up and grind. But I was sitting in a restaurant in Daytona, barely able to pay a dinner bill, and all that hard work had gotten me here.

The hardest thing about that moment wasn't the money. It was the mirror in the bathroom. Looking at myself after I received the check, and for the first time in my life thinking, should I just run out? No, I knew I was better than that. However, those intrusive thoughts, even for a second, showed me how low I was. Disgusted with myself and who I've become.

I walked back to the table, pulling out the few dollars I had left. Why did I choose to eat at one of the most expensive restaurants in Daytona? What was I thinking?

That's when he sat down.

An older white man. Didn't look like anyone I'd normally be around, more like a computer programmer or an old-school door-to-door vacuum salesman than anyone from the world I came from. He handed me a napkin for my tears, made a joke about the waitress waiting for me to ask for her number, and somehow made me laugh when I had nothing to laugh about.

He asked me if I was having a bad day or a terrible year.

I said day. Then I said, maybe two months. Then I said honestly, maybe a terrible year or two.

He nodded and said he remembered when he had a bad decade. And then he asked if I wanted to hear about it.

For the next 45 minutes, a man I had never met told me about the worst ten years of his life and how he turned it all around. And the word he used more than any other - more than strategy, more than money, more than opportunity - was discipline. Discipline this. With discipline, that. If you have discipline...

After 45 minutes, he handed me his business card and $200. He told me he was serious about the waitress. I never went to ask for her number.

But I called him the next morning. And then the morning after that. And then for the next ten years.

That man became my first mentor. And that night in Daytona Beach, Florida - broke, lost, sitting at a table I couldn't afford in a city I had driven to on nothing but desperation became the night I started becoming someone worth being.

I'm telling you this because I want you to know who wrote this book.

I wasn't born with discipline. Not someone who had it figured out early in life. Not a guy who read the right books and followed the right system and never struggled.

The principles in these pages didn't come from research. They came from losing a business I loved. Losing my football career and the only thing I ever truly wanted to be. From years of being the hardest worker in the room with nothing to show for it, because hard work without discipline is just exhaustion with good intentions.

The principles in this book came from a father who worked three jobs and never missed a game. A first mentor, Mr. T, who refused to accept mediocrity., influenced me. From a wife I had to become a completely different man to deserve. From a God who showed up in a restaurant in Daytona Beach when I had run out of everything else.

This book is what I know for certain. Not what I read somewhere. What I lived.

Let's get into it.

PART ONE- The Truth About Discipline

Chapter 1

THE MAN WHO TAUGHT ME EVERYTHING WITHOUT SAYING A WORD

My father never once sat me down and gave me a speech about discipline.

He didn't have to.

He worked three jobs at the same time for stretches of my childhood. Three jobs. And in all that time, all those early mornings and late nights, all that exhaustion I couldn't have understood as a kid, I cannot remember him missing a single football game or track meet. Not any of my brothers' and sisters' games either. He was there. Every time. In the stands. Present.

I found out years later, after I had kids of my own and could finally do the math, what some of those jobs actually cost him. Racist management. Coworkers who treated him in ways that today would shut a company down. Things he was required to do daily as part of his job description that would make your blood boil if I described them. He carried all of that. Every single day.

And he never brought it home.

Not once did we grow up hearing our father complain about work. Not once did we see him use what he was dealing with as a reason to check out, to be less present, to give less than everything to his family. He just showed up. To the jobs, games, and dinner table. To the life he had never once complained about.

That is discipline. Not the word. The life.

What he gave me was an incredible head-start. By the time I left high school, I was ready to outwork anyone. On the football field, in business, in anything I touched, I brought effort. I believed that if you just worked hard enough, long enough, it would be enough.

What I didn't understand yet, what took me years and a lot of pain to learn, was that my father already knew something I hadn't figured out yet. Hard work is the floor, not the ceiling. It gets you into the room. But it doesn't keep you there. It doesn't scale. It doesn't survive burnout. And it doesn't replace the knowledge, the discipline, and the personal growth required to expand beyond what you can carry on your back alone.

I came out of college, and by 25 I owned a business, had lived in four different states, was still playing football, driving a nice car, going to church every Sunday, and visiting my parents as much as I could. My father's foundation had set me up well. But I was like a computer that was originally built just to check emails and browse the web, and now someone expected it to edit videos, run a business, and game at the same time.

I needed to upgrade. I just didn't know it yet.

I kept working harder instead of working smarter. Sixteen-hour days, seven days a week, for years at a stretch. My employees were telling me about family vacations and weekend trips while I hadn't had an actual day off in longer than I could remember. I was running a gym and running it into the ground, not because I wasn't working, but because I had never taken a single business class, never learned financial management, never built systems that could carry the weight when I wasn't there to carry it myself.

Eventually, I burned out. And when you burn out without discipline to fall back on, what fills the space is procrastination. What follows procrastination is fear. What follows fear is excuses. And what follows excuses, if you let it run long enough, is failure.

I sold my gym for the lowest offer I received. It was the only one willing to pay quickly; I will touch more on why I needed this in a later chapter. Pennies compared to what they were worth. The competitor who bought it got the better end of that deal, and I knew it the moment I signed. I had built something I loved and planned to pass down to my children, and I let it go for what amounted to a moment of financial desperation and a complete absence of the discipline required to fight through it.

That was the cost.

But here's what I want you to understand about my father. He gave me the most important thing first. Grit. Work ethic. The understanding that showing up when you don't want to is not optional; it's the job. He just couldn't give me what he didn't have, which was the business knowledge, the systems thinking, the personal development tools that turn raw effort into lasting results.

He gave me the engine. I had to find the blueprints.

My father passed away in March 2025. I talked to him every single day of my life. When I say every day, I mean that literally; there was no week, no stretch, no period in my adult life when my father and I didn't speak. That daily call was as much a part of my routine as anything else in this book.

And then one day it wasn't there anymore.

The one thing I wish he had seen, more than the YouTube channel, more than the Amazon bestseller list, more than any of the external success, is how my relationship with God has grown. My father was a man of Christ. My father would have been most proud to see the man I am now and witness my family's return to the principles he raised me on.

He knew what I thought of him. I told him I loved him every single day. He knew.

But I want him to know this too: Dad, I finally understand what you were showing me. Every morning you got up and went to a job that didn't deserve you. And every weekend you showed up to our games on legs that had every right to be too tired to move. Every year you gave us a normal childhood while carrying so much stress we couldn't see.

You never called it discipline. You just lived it.

And if you had someone like him, this book is your chance to finally live up to what they showed you. If you didn't, this book is what they would have wanted you to know.

Chapter 2

NO ONE IS COMING TO FIX YOUR LIFE — THAT'S ACTUALLY GREAT NEWS

I spent a long time waiting for things to click. Waiting for the right moment. The right opportunity. The right amount of energy. I told myself I'd get it together when the timing was right. When life calmed down. When I had less on my plate.

That moment never came. And eventually I realized it was never going to.

There is no one else who will fix your schedule. No one is going to wake you up early. Nobody is coming to make you put the phone down, get off the couch, and do the work you keep saying you're going to do. Nobody's showing up at your door with a plan for your life. That's your job. It's always been your job.

I know that sounds harsh. But I'm not saying it to make you feel bad. I'm saying it because once you truly accept it, everything changes. When you stop waiting for someone else to make it happen, a boss, a spouse, a mentor, a sign from God, and you look at yourself in the mirror and say, "This is on me."

My first mentor didn't let me forget this. A few months into our calls, after I had spent plenty of time explaining all the reasons things hadn't gone the way I planned, he stopped me. He said the second I could accept that I wasn't where I wanted to be because I had a problem, not a circumstance problem, not a timing problem, not an economy problem, I could heal. I could learn. I could grow. But not until then.

Then he held up a mirror. I didn't want to look into. He pointed out that I had more success than most people I knew and that I had used that as an excuse to stop learning. What had that gotten me? A competitor bought a business I sold for pennies. A house that I was renting, not one that I owned. While I could barely make the monthly payment, I was driving a nice car to pretend to the world I was successful. Parents who had worked two and three jobs their whole lives and sacrificed everything, and I couldn't even cover their groceries for a year.

He didn't accept my mediocrity. And that is one of the greatest gifts anyone has ever given me.

That's what real accountability looks like. He prevented me from finding comfort in a story that held me captive. Most people around you will let you stay comfortable. They will find your excuses acceptable and validate your reasons. They'll tell you that you had it tough, and it wasn't your fault.

And maybe some of that is even true. But it doesn't matter. Because the truth that changes your life isn't who's to blame for where you are. It's who's responsible for where you go next.

That's you. Only you. And that's not a burden. That's freedom.

The world is full of people with real potential who are waiting. Waiting for permission, motivation, and for the stars to align. And while they wait, the people who decided to just start, messy, imperfect, scared, those are the ones getting somewhere.

I'm not talking about being a superhero. I'm not talking about grinding twenty hours a day. I'm talking about ownership. Looking at your life and saying Whatever this is, it's mine. And I'm the only one who can change it.

That's the starting line. And most people never get there.

No one is coming. And that's the best news you'll ever receive. Because it means everything that happens next is yours. The credit and the progress. The life. All of it is yours.

Chapter 3

MOTIVATION IS A LIAR. THIS IS WHAT ACTUALLY WORKS

People love to talk about motivation. They watch the videos, read the quotes, listen to the podcasts, and for about thirty minutes, they feel like they can conquer the world. Then they sit back down on the couch, and nothing changes.

That's because motivation is a feeling. And feelings come and go. You can't build a life on a feeling any more than you can build a house on sand.

I used to be addicted to motivation. Discovering Les Brown is a day I recall; he ignited my spirit in a way that hadn't happened in years. I shared his message with everyone around me. For three days straight, all I did was search for every speech he had ever given, re-listen to the ones I'd already heard, and burn his audio onto a CD so I could play it in my car on the way to work. I had plans. Big ones. People were aware of what I planned to do. I was determined to follow through.

Day four or five, something shifted. Life started doing what life does. A problem here. A distraction there. Fatigue. Obligation. The ordinary weight of a regular week. And Les Brown, the man whose words had felt like a fire in my chest seventy-two hours earlier, I couldn't even bring myself to press play. The CD sat in my car for weeks. The plans I had told people about went nowhere. I was right back to the uninspired version of myself, except now I also had to avoid the people I'd told.

The problem wasn't Les Brown. His message is genuine. The problem was that I was relying on a temporary emotion to drive permanent behavior. That never works. It can't work. Because the emotion always fades.

Think about what my father's life looked like. My dad wasn't waking up at 3 AM to go to a job that mistreated him because he watched a motivational video the night before. He wasn't dragging himself to a third job on a Saturday night because he felt inspired. He went because that's what the life he had chosen required. Because his family needed him to. Because he had decided, once, firmly, without constant renegotiation, that this is what a man does.

Motivation gets you started. Discipline gets you up every single day for fifty years to do something you don't want to do because it has to be done.

That's the difference. Motivation is a spark. Discipline is the furnace.

Discipline is a decision you make once, and then you reinforce it every single day through action. You don't decide every morning whether you're going to brush your teeth. You just do it. That's what discipline looks like when it's working. The things that matter become non-negotiable. You don't debate them. You just do them because that's who you are now.

The shift from motivation to discipline is the shift from I'll do it when I feel like it to I'll do it because I said I would. One of those builds a life. The other builds a collection of half-started projects and broken promises to yourself.

And every broken promise to yourself chips away at your self-trust. When you say you're going to wake up early and you don't, you're teaching yourself that your word means nothing. Do that enough times and you stop believing yourself altogether.

Discipline rebuilds that trust. One kept promise at a time. So make one today. Not tomorrow. Today. Keep it. That's how it starts.

Chapter 4

"I'll Start Monday" Is How Dreams Die on a Sunday Night

You know what Monday is? Monday is the most popular start date in the history of plans that never happen. Everyone is starting on Monday. New diets always start on Monday, along with the new workout plan to follow. New morning routine on Monday. Monday is the promised land of good intentions.

And then Monday comes. You hit snooze. Or something comes up. Or you're tired from the weekend. Therefore, it gets pushed to next Monday. And then the Monday after that. And before you know it, six months have gone by and you're still starting Monday.

I was a professional at this. And here's what made me so dangerous to myself: I was good at it. My excuses weren't lazy. They were airtight. The reason I constructed to wait was so logical, well-reasoned, and completely sensible that by the time I finished making the case in my head, I had convinced myself that starting tomorrow was actually the smarter move. I wasn't procrastinating. I was being strategic.

The reason was so good that , replaying it in my head, I convinced myself I was better off starting tomorrow.

That's the most sophisticated form of self-sabotage there is. When you're smart enough to lie to yourself convincingly.

Here's what "I'll start Monday" actually means. It means I don't want to do it right now. That's all. It's a way of giving yourself permission to keep doing nothing while still feeling like you have a plan. It's procrastination wearing a calendar.

I want to tell you about JW.

JW was my brother. Not by blood, but by everything else that actually makes someone family. We played college football together. He was a big guy, the size that makes sense on a football field and not for longevity, and after our playing days were done, neither of us was moving the way we should have been. He lived in New York. I was in Ohio and Virginia most of the time. And for a stretch of time that I will never stop wishing I could take back, he kept asking me to come visit.

He would call me, and the conversation always started the same way.

"When are you coming to New York, son?"

"Soon, JW. I'll be there soon."

"That's what you said last month, B."

He wasn't wrong. He was never wrong about that.

One afternoon he called with something specific on his mind.

"When you come up here, son, we should run the NYC Marathon together."

"JW. I am not a runner. They will need to call an ambulance for me somewhere around mile thirteen."

"We can train for it. Whoever finishes first, the other one has to pay their car insurance for a year."

"Do you even have a car? I thought you New Yorkers all took taxis."

JW laughed. Loud. The way he always did, even when the joke wasn't that good.

"I got a car. And insurance up here is stupid high. Stop listening to the movies, so I suggest you train, B."

That was how we talked. We joked, always called each other out; it was always a bet and always something to look forward to that we never quite got to.

He said other things too, in that same calm tone, things I heard as jokes because that's how we talk to each other.

"When you come, maybe you can help me with my diet. I'm trying to get as skinny as you, Son."

"Get here and I'll let you drag me up a flight of stairs. Maybe two if you're lucky."

Listen, JW took the elevator if it's an option, and if the building only had stairs, he would tell us I will stay in the car. He hated stairs.

I had every personal training certification available. More education and knowledge about the human body than most people in any room I walked into. And I heard those words as jokes because I wasn't paying close enough attention to hear what was underneath them.

I kept saying, next week. Next Monday, I'm coming. I'll be there soon.

One day I finally went. I picked up the phone to call him and let him know I was booking the flight. I was actually already there to surprise him. He lived in New Jersey at this point with his brother; they had just moved out of NY and both found good jobs in Jersey.

His older brother answered. He died this morning.

JW was gone. A heart condition none of us knew about. His friends, not family. They all knew.

I have felt broken about that for over twenty years. I am still broken about it now.

Looking back, I can see every signal I missed from the marathon idea, the stairs joke, the diet comment. He wasn't just reaching out as a friend, making conversation. He was reaching out as a man who needed help and didn't know how to ask for it directly, because men rarely do. Especially with our friends, we exhibit excessive pride. We don't want to show how sick we are. We don't want to be the ones who need saving. So we wrap it in a joke and hope that someone who loves us is paying close enough attention to hear what's underneath it.

I wasn't paying attention.

In my father's last hours, before we brought him home for hospice care, his best friend came to the hospital. My father could barely speak. The life had been slowly leaving his body for days, and everyone in that room knew it. But when his best friend walked through that door, my father sat up in that bed and talked to him. Everything felt normal for approximately five minutes. Like the man we knew was still fully there.

Men don't show each other how sick they are. Not until they absolutely have to. And sometimes by then it's too late for anything except five minutes that feel like a miracle.

This is a significant part of why I do what I do now. The YouTube channel. The podcast. This book. I have lost too many people to health and to silence and to the false promise of more time. A walking encyclopedia of fitness and nutrition, and I still couldn't find the right words to help the people I loved most before it was too late. Not because I didn't have the knowledge. Because I wasn't there. Because I kept waiting for a better time that never came.

The things I pushed to Monday. The decisions, the actions, the visits, the conversations that I'll never get back. That's the actual cost of "I'll start Monday" that nobody tells you about. It's not just today that you're losing. It's the compound effect of all the today's you keep trading away for a future that never arrives. And sometimes that future takes someone with it.

Disciplined people don't wait for Monday. They start now. Even if it's Wednesday at 2 PM and they just had a bad lunch. They start where they are with what they have and figure the rest out as they go.

If you're reading this right now and there's something you've been putting off, do one small piece of it before you go to sleep tonight. Not the whole thing.

Monday is a lie. Today is all you've got. Everything is a today problem. Because sometimes tomorrow doesn't come, and the only thing left is the weight of all the Mondays you never kept.

Do it now: Before you turn this page, do one thing. Right now. Not tomorrow. Think of the one thing you've been putting off until Monday and do the first step of it before you go to sleep tonight. Make the call. Write the first sentence. Book the flight. One step. Tonight. Monday just became today.

Chapter 5

YOU ALREADY KNOW WHAT TO DO. SO WHY HAVEN'T YOU DONE IT?

Most people don't have an information problem. They have an action problem.

You already know you should eat better. Your body needs more movement, and you know that too. Spending less time on your phone, going to bed earlier, saving more money, being more present with your family, stopping the habit of putting off the things that matter. None of that is new information. You have known all of it for a long time.

You don't need another book to tell you what you already know. The problem is you are consuming information as a substitute for doing something with it.

There was a stretch in my life where I read every book I could get my hands on. Zig Ziglar's *Born to Win*. James Allen's *As a Man Thinketh*. Les Brown's *Live Your Dreams*. Og Mandino's *The Greatest Salesman in the World*. Marcus Aurelius and his *Meditations*. The Bible. I was going after all of it, underlining passages, filling up notebooks, memorizing quotes. And underneath every page I turned was the same driving force. I wanted to become a millionaire. That was the goal. That was the whole point.

I was building a library and calling it a plan.

Every book I finished felt like progress. Every highlighted passage felt like a step forward. I could talk about mindset, purpose, and the power of thought with genuine conviction because I had read everything on the subject. What I could not do was look at my bank account and explain where all that money, I mean wisdom, had gone. The books were piling up on my shelf. The money was not stacking up anywhere. My daily habits, my decisions, my follow-through, none of it had changed. I had consumed enough information to fill a curriculum, and I was still the same man making the same choices every single day.

That is when I understood what those books were actually doing for me. They were making me feel like I was becoming someone without requiring me to do anything differently. Reading about discipline is comfortable. Living it is not. Reading about the millionaire mindset is easy. Building something that generates real wealth is years of unglamorous work that no highlight reel and no book prepares you for. I was using influential books written by prominent leaders as a substitute for the one thing none of them could do for me, which was to act.

Collecting ideas like trophies. Proud of what I knew. Blind to the fact that knowing had changed nothing.

Knowledge without action is entertainment. It makes you feel productive without actually producing anything. And it is dangerous because it tricks you into thinking you are moving forward when you are really just standing still with better vocabulary.

Mr. T called this out early in our work together. He told me I thought I knew everything because I had more visible success than most people around me, and I had used that as a reason to stop growing. What had all that knowing actually gotten me? A competitor bought the business for pennies. A car I could barely afford. Parents who had sacrificed everything, and a son who could not cover their groceries.

The knowing was never the problem. The doing was.

Discipline closes the gap between knowing and doing. That is its entire job.

Here is a test. Think about the one thing in your life you most want to change. Now ask yourself honestly: do you not know how to change it, or do you just not want to do what it takes? Nine times out of ten, you know exactly what needs to happen. You have known for a while. You have not done it yet.

Stop researching. Stop planning. Stop waiting until you feel ready enough.

You are ready. You have been ready. Go do the thing.

Chapter 6

YOUR FEELINGS ARE LYING TO YOU EVERY SINGLE DAY

This might be the most important chapter in this book, so pay attention.

You are going to feel like quitting. You are going to feel tired, frustrated, unmotivated, distracted, and overwhelmed. And when those feelings show up, and they will, you need to understand one thing. Feelings are not instructions.

Just because you feel like staying in bed doesn't mean you should stay in bed. Just because you feel like eating garbage doesn't mean you should eat garbage. Feeling like scrolling your phone for another hour doesn't make it the right call. Your feelings are loud. They are convincing. And they are wrong more often than you think.

We live in a culture that tells us to follow our feelings. Do what feels right. Follow your heart. If it doesn't feel good, it's not for you. And I understand the spirit behind that. But for discipline, that advice will destroy you. Because the things that build a good life almost never feel good in the moment. They feel hard; they feel boring and they feel inconvenient. That's the point. If discipline felt easy, everybody would have it.

Working out feels hard. Saving money instead of spending it feels limiting. Having a tough conversation with your spouse feels uncomfortable. Waking up early feels terrible. But every single one of those things improves your life. And every time you choose the easy, feel-good option, you are trading your future for a moment of relief.

Let me tell you about the early days of my YouTube channel.

When I finally started it, my first subscriber was my wife. Not a stranger who found the content valuable. My wife. Out of loyalty. It took several days before a second person subscribed, and that person was probably also someone who knew me personally. The numbers were so small. The validation was that absent.

I had been giving people this same information face to face for years. In gyms, in masterminds, one on one with people who needed help. I knew this material cold. Put a camera in front of me, and something happened that I still find hard to fully explain. I froze. I looked like I didn't belong talking about the very things I had spent decades learning. The confidence I carried into every room I walked into disappeared the moment that lens pointed at my face.

I scheduled YouTube videos on my calendar and blew them off. Repeatedly. The feelings were overwhelming and specific. I don't know how to edit. I look stupid on screen. Nobody is watching anyway. What is the point? Every excuse felt completely reasonable because something real tied it down. The discomfort, awkwardness, and slow growth were real.

But here is what I have learned from being on the other side of it now, and from watching hundreds of other creators either push through or walk away. Those who build something never say they would try it and see what happens. That mindset is a trap because it gives you a permanent exit ramp. Every hard day becomes a reason to use it.

Those who created something understood the challenges ahead, committed to persevere until they improved, and consistently appeared on camera, exposing their awkwardness to the public. The subscribers were never the point. The ad revenue was never the point. Making quality content and trusting the process was the point. Everything else is a bonus that comes later, long after most people have already quit.

YouTube is one of the hardest things I have ever done consistently. And it is also one of the clearest examples I have of what happens when you refuse to let your feelings make your decisions. Every video I did not feel like making but made anyway is the reason this channel exists today. Every morning I scheduled a shoot and wanted to cancel but didn't is a brick in something real.

Your feelings told me not to turn the camera on. Discipline told me to do it, anyway. You are reading this book in part because I listened to discipline instead.

That's what discipline is. The ability to separate what you feel from what you do.

The more you practice that the stronger you get. Not just physically. Mentally. You build a version of yourself that neither a bad mood nor a rough morning can derail. The feelings still show up. They always show up. You just stop letting them vote on what happens next.

Your feelings will lie to you every single day. Discipline tells the truth.

Chapter 7

COMFORT IS COSTING YOU EVERYTHING (AND YOU CAN'T SEE THE BILL)

Comfort is expensive. Not in dollars. In what it takes from you. Every time you choose comfort over growth, you are paying a price you will not see on a receipt. And the bill comes due later, when you look around and realize you are in the same place you were a year ago. Three years ago. Five years ago.

This is not about relaxation. Rest is necessary, and we will get to that. This is about the habit of always choosing the easier path. When selecting the path of least effort, discomfort, and risk. Over time, that pattern does not keep you safe. It keeps you stuck.

For a couple of years my mentor kept pushing me toward things I kept finding cheaper, easier ways around. He would tell me about a seminar I should attend, and I would look at the price and think, this will be on YouTube soon enough. He would recommend a book and tell me he could not wait to see how marked up my copy was, the way his was when he first read it. I would think I will just get the audiobook. I cannot sit with three hundred pages.

I told myself I was being practical. I was comfortable. There is a difference, and I did not want to see it.

Then one day, while I was living in Florida and working at a luxury hotel full-time while trying to figure out my business on the side, I ran into an old college friend. We had not seen each other for about ten years. He was traveling as a guest of the hotel. We started talking, and I asked him what he had been up to.

What he had been up to was building a multimillion-dollar gym franchise.

"How did you get here?" I asked him.

"Tony Robbins," he said. "I attended a couple of his live events. Changed everything for me. Woke up something I didn't know was asleep."

Then he reached into his bag and pulled out three books he was currently reading. He had marked up every single book so heavily that it looked less like the author's work and more like his own personal manuscript. Notes in the margins. Highlighted passages. Dog-eared pages. These were not books he had read. These were books he had lived in.

I stood there looking at those books and felt something shift.

Everything Mr. T had been trying to get me to do for two years was standing right in front of me in that hotel lobby. Not as advice. As evidence. My old friend had not gotten where he was by finding the cheaper version of growth or waiting for the audiobook.

I was not ready to hear it from my mentor. God knew that. So he sent someone else to show me what I needed to see. God sent someone I respected to my hotel. Someone whose results I could not argue with. Someone I had not seen in ten years and would not see again for fifteen more. A brief appearance that served one purpose and then was gone.

After that conversation, everything changed. My book consumption has increased from hardly any per year to approximately fifty. My car listening habits have changed from music to lectures, interviews, and educational content. I watched YouTube differently, not for entertainment but for information I could use. I stopped looking for the discounted version of growth and started paying the actual price for it.

And here is what I learned. Comfort is addictive. The more you have, the more you need. Your tolerance for discomfort goes down quietly, without announcing itself, until things that used to feel normal feel hard. Your baseline keeps shifting until the smallest inconvenience feels unbearable. I had been comfortable for so long that even sitting with a book felt like too much to ask of myself before my old friend showed up.

Discipline is the antidote. It keeps your tolerance for discomfort high. It reminds your body and your mind that you are capable of hard things. Not because you enjoy them, but because you refuse to let comfort make your decisions.

To me, discipline is like getting a call that the best boxers in the world want to meet you at 4 PM to fight, and you show up anyway. You show up to your own beat-down because showing up is the whole point.

That is the standard. Not showing up when it is easy. Showing up when you already know what it is going to cost you.

The question is never whether you can afford to be uncomfortable. The question is whether you can afford what comfort has already quietly taken from you.

PART TWO — Daily Discipline

Chapter 8

Win the Morning or Spend the Day Playing Catch-Up

How you start your morning sets the tone for your entire day. It's not the 9 AM meeting. Not the email you sent at noon. Not the decision you make at 3 PM when your brain is running on fumes. The first thirty minutes after you open your eyes set the tone. Everything else is downstream from that.

I didn't always believe that. I used to think morning routines were for people with too much free time. People who could afford to sit around journaling and meditating before the sun came up. Then I looked honestly at what my mornings actually looked like and realized the problem wasn't that I didn't have time for a routine. The problem was that my routine was destroying me, and I hadn't noticed.

For years my morning looked like this. Alarm at 8 AM. Coffee before a single drop of water had touched my lips. Phone in hand before my feet hit the floor, scrolling social media, checking emails, firing off replies, consuming everyone else's agenda before I had even decided what mine was. By 8:45 I was out the door, already behind, already reactive, already giving the best of my mental energy to things that had nothing to do with my life or my own goals. I thought I was being productive. What I was actually doing was starting every day by handing my focus to everyone else and calling it a morning.

That version of me arrived everywhere already depleted. Already behind. Already on defense. And I carried that energy into every conversation, every decision, and every opportunity the day offered. You cannot show up full for your life when you spent the first hour of your day emptying yourself out for everyone else.

The shift started with a book.

In 2016, I read United by United States Senator Cory Booker. In it, he described a group of men he met with regularly, early in the morning, to talk about life, faith, leadership, and how to show up better for their communities. Not a restaurant club. Not anything fancy. Just a small circle of committed people who understood that the early morning hours belonged to the things that mattered most, before the demands of the day crowded them out.

I read that and thought; I need that.

So I built it. I reached out to a group of men I trusted, all of whom I considered friends, and proposed a mastermind. A regular gathering where we could pour into each other, hold each other accountable, and talk about the things men rarely talk about openly. The only problem was finding a time that worked for everyone. These were busy men with jobs, families, and responsibilities. We went back and forth trying to find a window that fit everyone's schedule.

The only time that worked was 5 AM.

It was wake up early, or the mastermind did not happen. And the mastermind mattered too much to let die over a preference for sleeping in. So I adjusted. I restructured my entire morning around that commitment, and in doing so, I discovered something that no one could have told me and made me believe. The early morning hours are the most valuable hours of the day. Not because they are magical. Because they are yours before anyone else can claim them.

That mastermind taught me that my old morning routine could not serve the life I was trying to build. I did not need more time. I needed to protect the time I already had and use it with intention before the world woke up and started making demands on it.

Here is what I want you to understand. You already have a morning routine. Everybody does. The only question is whether yours is working for you or against you. Waking up and grabbing your phone is a routine. Hitting snooze three times is a routine. Coffee before water, email before intention, reaction before thought, all of that is a routine. It is just one that is costing you every single day without sending you a bill.

The morning I have now looks nothing like that.

I wake up and the first thing I do is thank God for a new day. Not formally. Not with a script. Just acknowledgment. Gratitude that there is another chance to get it right. From there, I drink a full liter of water before anything else enters my body. Your body wakes up dehydrated every single morning. Water before coffee is not a preference. It is maintenance. Give your body what it actually needs before you give it what you want.

Then I sit with my journal and write. Getting out of my head and onto the page, whatever needs to come out. You do not need to be a writer to journal. You need to be a person whose thoughts are cluttering your mind and slowing you down. The page takes them out of your head and puts them somewhere you can see them. That alone changes how clearly you think for the rest of the day. A few pages from whatever book I am currently reading follow the journal. Something to feed my mind before the noise of the day competes for space in it.

Then I train. 45 minutes in my home gym. By the time I am done, my body is awake, my mind is sharp, and I have already done something hard before most people have opened their eyes. There is a confidence that comes from that. A quiet one. Nobody gives you a trophy for your 5 AM workout. But you know. And that knowledge changes how you carry yourself for the rest of the day.

After training, I wake my kids and cook them breakfast. That sequence matters more than it might sound. I am not stumbling into their morning half-present and already stressed. I am showing up for them full. Ready. My oldest son is usually already up with me by that point, absorbing the routine without either of us ever having a conversation about it. That is how discipline gets passed down. Not through speeches. Through what they see you do before the world wakes up.

While the kids are eating, my wife and I take fifteen minutes and walk outside together to check on our garden. We get the morning sun hitting us directly, and that is not a small thing. Morning sunlight within the first hour of waking up regulates your body's internal clock, improves your mood, sharpens your focus, and sets your energy for the entire day. Most people are inside under artificial light, wondering why they feel sluggish by noon. Ten to fifteen minutes of direct morning sun will do more for your energy and mental clarity than a second cup of coffee ever could.

The walk's purpose is not to produce output. It is fifteen minutes of presence with the person I built my life with, outside, in the quiet of the early morning before the day pulls us in different directions. Protect something like that in your own morning. It does not have to be a garden. It does not have to be with a spouse. But find something in your routine that exists purely because it feeds you as a person, not because it makes you more productive. Those minutes make the productive ones sustainable.

Then, and only then, I have my coffee. And it is delicious in a way that coffee grabbed in a rush while scrolling on a phone never was.

I also talk to God during those early hours. Not formally. Just conversation. The same way I used to call my father every single day, just checking in, expressing gratitude, asking for guidance, reminding myself who I am doing all of this for. That spiritual grounding changes how I carry everything that comes after it. Whatever that anchor looks like for you, faith, meditation, stillness, silence, build it into your morning. Starting your day connected to something larger than your to-do list changes the quality of everything on that list.

Now here is the part where you stop reading and start thinking about your own morning.

What is the first thing you do when you wake up? Be honest. Is that your phone? Or maybe coffee before water? Is it email before intention? Is it stumbling into the day without a single moment that belongs to you?

You do not need to copy my routine. You need to build yours. Start with these three things and work from there.

First, do not touch your phone for the first thirty minutes of your morning. Not for anything. Let those thirty minutes belong entirely to you before you let the world in.

Second, drink water before coffee. Your body has been without hydration for seven or eight hours. Give it what it needs first.

Third, go outside and get morning sunlight on your face for at least ten minutes. Walk. Sit. Stand. It does not matter. Just get outside and let the light hit you before you sit under fluorescent bulbs and wonder why you feel half awake all day.

Build from there. Add what fits your life. Remove what doesn't. But start somewhere intentional and protect it like it matters. Because it does.

A morning routine is not about luxury. It is about deciding, before the chaos starts, who is in control of your day. The world will take every minute that you do not claim for yourself. Your phone will take them; your email will take them along with obligations to family and business. The only way to keep them is to wake up with a plan and execute it before anyone else gets a vote.

Senator Booker's breakfast club was never really about breakfast. It was about a group of people who understood that the way you start your day determines the person you are by the end. That idea changed my life. Build your own version of it. Find your 5 AM people if you need accountability. Start walking in your garden; if you need stillness. Find your water and your journal and your quiet conversation with God before the noise begins.

The morning belongs to the disciplined. Everybody else is just reacting.

Chapter 9

THE ONE TASK YOU KEEP AVOIDING IS THE ONLY ONE THAT MATTERS TODAY

I know what it feels like to avoid the hardest thing. Not for a day. For months.

When my gym started going under, I knew before anyone else did. I took out loans to keep the lights on and meet payroll. I was doing it quietly, by myself, carrying that weight every single day while my staff showed up, did their jobs, and trusted that everything was fine. Because from where they were standing, it looked fine.

I kept telling myself I would figure it out. That something would turn around. So I kept going. Kept showing up. Kept avoiding the one conversation that needed to happen.

The day I finally sat my small staff of five down was one of the hardest days of my life. These were not just employees. I knew their families. I knew what their paychecks meant to them. I knew which ones were paying rent with that money, which ones were putting their kids through school, which ones were counting on that income to put groceries on the table. I had built something with these people and I had let it get to a place where I had to look them in the eyes and tell them that in 90 days the gym would close its doors for good.

Think about what that feels like from their side. You show up to work one day thinking everything is fine. Your boss calls a meeting. Then you find out that in 90 days you need a new job. That the thing you were counting on is gone. That is what I put my staff through because I kept avoiding the hard conversation for months, hoping I would never have to have it.

The conversation did not get easier because I waited. It got harder. Every month I delayed was another month my staff could have been updating their resumes, networking, and preparing for what was coming.

Instead, they were in the dark because I could not bring myself to do the hard thing when it needed to be done.

The gym did eventually close. A competitor bought it, and what I received from that sale was nowhere near what it was worth. Pennies compared to what I had built. But I decided about those pennies. I divided most of what I received and gave it to my staff as a final bonus. Not because I was required to. Because I owed them that much. It was enough to give each of them a three to six month financial cushion while they figured out their next move.

It wasn't enough to make up for what happened. But it was the right thing to do. And doing the right thing at the end does not erase the cost of avoiding the hard thing at the beginning. My staff deserved that conversation months before they got it. The money I gave them helped. The time I took from them I can never give back.

That is what avoidance costs. Not just you. The surrounding people.

Here is the truth about hard tasks. They do not shrink while you wait. They grow. Every day you push the hard thing to tomorrow, you are adding weight to it. The conversation that would have taken ten minutes in January takes an hour in March and costs you everything by June. Avoidance is not rest. It is debt. And like all debt, it collects interest.

Whatever the hardest task on your list is today, do it first. Not a second. Not after you check your email, organize your desk, or handle the things that feel productive but do not move the needle. Do the hard thing first because your mental energy and willpower are at their peak in the morning. As the day goes on, both get drained by small decisions, interruptions, and the ordinary friction of being alive. Trying to tackle your hardest task at 3 PM is like trying to sprint the last mile of a marathon. You might finish, but you will not do your best work, and you know it.

Now I flip it. The first task of my day is the one I least want to do. Every single time I start it, I find the same thing waiting for me on the other side of starting. It was never as bad as I built it up to be. The dread was heavier than the actual work. But you only discover that by doing it. No amount of reading about it will convince you. Start and find out for yourself.

Stop saving the hard stuff for later. Later never comes.

Do it first. Free yourself. And stop making the people around you pay for what you keep avoiding.

Chapter 10

15 Minutes a Day Will Change Your Life (Do the Math)

One of the biggest lies people believe about discipline is that you need hours. And because they don't have hours, they don't start.

Fifteen minutes is enough. If that's all you've got, take it.

I know this personally because there was a season where I had lost the love for fitness. Not the knowledge. Not the discipline. The love. I used to live in my gym seven days a week, two hours a day. That was my life. Then the fourth kid came. The business was growing. The time I used to pour into training started disappearing, and I didn't know how to work out in the margins. I only knew how to go all in. And when all in wasn't available anymore, I was going nowhere.

I remember telling my wife that I wanted to build an outdoor gym. We didn't have the money for it. So I looked around at what I already had and thought, all the equipment I need is right here.

Walking lunges before I check on my plants. Pushups in the grass. Sandbags I lift and carry through the garden rows. I was already going to be outside for thirty minutes checking on things. Adding fifteen minutes of movement onto that wasn't a sacrifice. It was just math.

What I discovered is that fifteen minutes outdoors with no distractions, fresh air, and sunlight changes everything about the quality of the work. Because I knew it was only fifteen minutes, I left nothing on the table. That became the best workout of my day. I check my Garmin watch after those sessions and I'm burning anywhere between 100 and 350 calories and getting over 100 quality reps in. When I do this twice, my morning walkthrough and my evening check, I've strung together thirty minutes of isolated training without even counting all the walking, lifting, and bending that gardening itself provides.

I still strength train three times a week. Bench, squat, deadlift, the fundamentals. This outdoor routine does not replace that. But it gave me something the indoor gym couldn't give me during that season of life. Momentum. A way back to the love of fitness when I thought I had lost it for good.

What started as a personal solution has now helped hundreds of backyard gardeners reimagine their outdoor space and reclaim time they said they didn't have. People who said they had no equipment. People who felt exactly the way I felt when that fourth kid came and the hours disappeared. Fifteen minutes in the garden changed all of that.

But here's what I need you to understand. This isn't just about fitness.

My wife and I went to Rome for our honeymoon. It was the best trip abroad we had ever taken. The people, the food, the history, all of it was extraordinary. But it was the language that got under my skin. There is something about Italian that sounds like music even when someone is arguing. I came home wanting to learn it.

Did I?

For about a month. Then life showed up, and it quietly disappeared the way things do when you haven't built the discipline to protect them yet.

Fast forward several years. Different man. Better habits. Stronger discipline. I committed to learning Italian, and this time I used the Power 15 to do it. Fifteen minutes every day, no phone, no distractions, fully present for every one of those minutes.

Here is what I noticed. When I used to sit down for thirty minutes to study, maybe five minutes I was actually engaged. The other twenty-five I was half present, drifting, checking something, losing the thread. Fifteen focused minutes produced more real learning than thirty distracted ones ever did. The language is coming. Slowly and consistently, the way everything worth building comes.

Italian is not the most important thing on my daily list. Keeping the lights on matters more. Time with my family matters more. But it matters to me. It is something I want for myself and for my wife, and the Power 15 gives me the time to pursue it, taking nothing away from the things that have to come first.

That is the real value of fifteen focused minutes. It creates space for the things that matter to you personally without requiring you to sacrifice the things that matter most. You do not have to choose between your responsibilities and your growth. Fifteen minutes carves out room for both.

People underestimate what fifteen minutes a day adds up to because they are thinking about it in isolation. Fifteen minutes today doesn't feel like much. But fifteen minutes a day, five days a week, for a year? That is over 65 hours. Sixty-five hours of building something. Learning something. Becoming something. That changes a life.

The trap is all-or-nothing thinking. If I can't do it perfectly, I won't do it at all. That is not discipline. That is ego.

I didn't have a perfect setup when I started. All I had was a garden, some sandbags, and fifteen minutes. I didn't have a language school or an immersive program. I had an app, a quiet room, and fifteen minutes. That was enough. It has always been enough.

Everyone has fifteen minutes. If you genuinely feel you don't, that is not a time problem. That is a priority problem. And that is worth sitting with, honestly.

Now think about your own life for a moment. What is the thing you keep saying you will get to when you have more time? What skill do you want to build? The language you want to learn. The project that keeps getting pushed to the back of the line. You do not need more time. You need fifteen minutes and the discipline to protect them.

Discipline is humble enough to take what's available and make the most of it.

Fifteen minutes. No phone. Full focus. Start today. And watch what happens.

The Power 15 Challenge: For the next seven days, set a timer for fifteen minutes every morning. No phone. No distractions. Pick one thing that matters to you. Could be fitness, a skill, a project, anything, and give it everything you have for those fifteen minutes. Just seven days. See what happens.

Chapter 11

STOP GOING HARD. START SHOWING UP. HERE'S THE DIFFERENCE.

Everybody wants to go hard. One massive workout or an intense week of clean eating. One all-nighter to finish the project. People love the sprint. It feels dramatic. It feels productive. And then they burn out and disappear for two weeks, wondering why nothing is changing.

Here is the truth nobody wants to hear. Intensity is a feeling. Consistency is a decision. And the decision always wins.

The person who does a little every day will always outpace the person who goes hard once and then vanishes. Consistently. Not sometimes. Not usually.. Because you don't build progress when you're fired up. Progress builds itself in the ordinary moments when you show up anyway, do the work, and go home. Day after day after day until the results become undeniable.

Stop chasing intensity. Start protecting consistency. Here is exactly what that looks like across every area of your life that actually matters.

In Your Fitness

Three hours at the gym on Saturday followed by six days on the couch is not a fitness routine. It is a performance. Your body does not adapt to occasional effort. It adapts to repeated stimuli. Twenty minutes of movement every morning will produce better results than a single brutal session once a week because your body is constantly being asked to improve rather than occasionally being shocked and then abandoned.

You do not need a perfect workout. You need a consistent one. Ten minutes of bodyweight exercises in your backyard counts. A twenty-minute walk before work counts. The standard is not how hard you go. The standard is whether you showed up. Set a minimum you can hit on your worst day and do that minimum every single day. On your best days, you will exceed it. On your hardest days, you will hit it, and that will be enough. Consistency lives in the minimum, not the maximum.

The garden teaches this better than any gym ever could. Ignore your plants for ten days and spend a whole Saturday trying to catch up, and you will find weeds that have taken over, something that died because you were not there to catch it, and a mess that one afternoon cannot fix. Show up for ten minutes every day, and your garden stays healthy, manageable, and ahead. Consistency keeps you in control. Intensity puts you in recovery mode. Choose accordingly.

In Your Relationships

Nobody falls out of love in a single day. Nobody loses their relationship with their child overnight. Those things erode slowly, quietly, through a thousand small moments where someone chose something else instead.

Consistency in relationships does not require grand gestures. It requires daily attention. An actual conversation with your spouse every single day, not about logistics, not about schedules, but about something that actually matters. Eye contact. Putting the phone face down and being fully present for fifteen minutes. Asking your kid one genuine question every day and actually listening to the answer without planning your response while they are still talking.

These things do not feel significant in the moment. They feel ordinary. That is exactly the point. Ordinary repeated daily becomes the foundation that holds everything together when life gets hard. The couples who survive difficulties are not the ones who had the biggest romantic gestures. They are the ones who showed up for each other in the small moments consistently enough that the relationship could handle the weight of the hard ones.

Cramming connection into one big talk once a year does not build trust. One genuine conversation every day does. Start tonight.

In Your Business

The overnight success you admire on social media is almost never overnight. Behind every business that appears to blow up suddenly are years of consistent, unglamorous work that nobody was watching and nobody was applauding. The content that nobody liked and the emails that nobody opened. Foundations for everything else came from those unnoticed efforts, which included days that seemed like a complete waste of time.

Consistency in business means doing the work whether the results are visible. It means posting the content when nobody is watching. Emailing when nobody is responding. Making the call when nobody is calling back. Building a skill when nobody is paying you for it yet. The market rewards people who show up long enough to get good and stay good, not people who sprint for sixty days and then reassess.

Pick the one thing in your business that compounds over time and do it every single day without negotiating with yourself about whether today is a good day for it. Write the post. Make the call. Send the pitch. Record the video. Do it today and do it again tomorrow. The results will come on their own timeline. Your job is to still be standing and still be working when they arrive.

In Your Finances

Financial consistency is the least exciting topic in personal development and also one of the most life-changing. Nobody gets wealthy from one great month. Nobody builds security from one big decision. You build wealth the same way you build everything else worth having: through small, disciplined actions you repeat consistently over a long period.

Twenty dollars into savings every paycheck will not make you rich this year. Over ten years, it builds a habit, a buffer, and a foundation that most people never have because they were waiting until they had more money to be intentional about the money they already had. The amount is not the point. The consistency is.

Track your spending every single week. Not monthly. Weekly. The month is too long. By the time you review it, you've already done the damage, and you've already set the pattern. Weekly tracking keeps you honest in real time when you can still adjust. Set one financial boundary this week that you did not have last week. Cancel a subscription you don't really need. One meal cooked instead of ordered. With impulse purchases, delay 24 hours to see if you still want it. Stack those small decisions consistently and watch what happens to your financial life over the next twelve months.

Discipline with money is not about being cheap. It is about being consistent with intention. Every dollar you spend unconsciously is a dollar that was not working toward the life you say you want.

Here is what all four have in common. None of them require you to be exceptional. None of them require perfect conditions or unlimited time, or a complete life overhaul. They require you to show up every day and do something small with intention.

The sprint feels good. The consistent daily effort feels ordinary. But ordinary done every day becomes extraordinary. That is not motivation. That is math.

Stop trying to be intense. Start being consistent. Intensity impresses people for a moment. Consistency builds a life.

Chapter 12

Your Phone Is Stealing Hours From You Every Day — Check the Receipts

Before you read another word, do one thing. Open your phone and check your screen time from the past week. Look at the daily average and at which apps are consuming the most of it. Look at how many times you picked up your phone yesterday.

Now sit with that number honestly.

Most people have somewhere between three and six hours of daily screen time. That is not a judgment. That is a national average backed by research, and it is worth understanding what it actually means in real terms. Three hours a day is 21 hours a week. That is nearly a full day every single week spent looking at a screen. Six hours a day is 42 hours a week. That is a full-time job's worth of your attention going somewhere other than your own life every seven days.

Now think about what you say you do not have time for. Working out. Reading. Cooking a proper meal. Being present with your kids. Building something that matters. Learning a skill. Starting the project. Having the conversation. The hours are there. Something that is not serving you already spoken for them.

Your phone is not neutral. They did not design it to improve your life. It captured your attention and held it for as long as possible because your attention is the product being sold to advertisers. Every notification engineers an interruption for you. The scrolling never ends. Engineers design every auto-play video to ensure you watch for an extended period, minute after minute. The people who built these platforms are among the most intelligent engineers and behavioral scientists alive, and they spent years perfecting the mechanisms that make it nearly impossible to put the device down. You are not weak for struggling with this. You are human. But understanding what you are up against is the first step toward doing something about it.

Here is what chronic phone use is actually costing you beyond the hours.

It is costing you your focus. Every time you pick up your phone and put it back down, your brain pays a refocusing tax. Research shows it takes an average of twenty-three minutes to return to deep focus after an interruption. If you are checking your phone several times an hour, you are not working between checks. You are recovering from them. The work you think you are doing in between notifications is significantly lower quality than the work you could do if the phone were not in the room at all.

It is costing you your relationships. Phubbing is the term researchers use for snubbing someone in favor of your phone, and studies show it damages relationship satisfaction even when the person on the receiving end says nothing about it. Your spouse notices when you reach for your phone while they are talking. Your kids notice when your eyes drift to the screen while they are telling you something. They may not say it out loud, but they are filing it away. Presence is one of the most valuable things you can give the people you love, and the phone is the single most common thing stealing it.

It is costing you your mental health. Passive social media consumption, where people scroll through others' highlight reels without creating or connecting, consistently links to increased anxiety, lower self-esteem, and decreased life satisfaction. You already know this on some level. You have felt it. That vague dissatisfaction after thirty minutes of scrolling that is hard to name but impossible to ignore. That is not an accident. It is the predictable result of spending time in an environment engineered to make you feel that you are missing out on something.

It is costing you your sleep. The blue light emitted by screens suppresses melatonin production and delays your body's natural sleep onset. Checking your phone within an hour of bedtime is not unwinding. It is neurologically activating. The content you consume before sleep, news, social media, arguments in comment sections, primes your nervous system for alertness rather than rest. Poor sleep degrades every other area of your life. Your mood. Your decision-making, discipline, and ability to show up for the people and the work that matter most.

Now, here is the practical part. Discipline with your phone is not about throwing it in a river. It is about being intentional with something that was specifically designed to prevent intentional use. Here is a system that works.

Start your morning. Do not touch your phone for the first thirty minutes after you wake up. Those first thirty minutes set the neurological tone for your entire day. Starting them in a reactive mode by immediately consuming other people's content and other people's demands hands control of your morning to everyone except you. Own the first thirty minutes. The phone will still be there.

Create phone-free **zones.** The dinner table is non-negotiable. The bedroom is worth serious consideration. Your car when you are with your family is another one. These are not punishments. These are protected spaces. In them, the people and experiences that genuinely matter to you receive your undivided attention, unlike the divided attention a phone provides.

Turn off nonessential notifications. Every notification is a request for your attention that you did not consent to. Go through your settings today and turn off every notification that does not require an immediate response. Email can wait. Social media can wait. The news can wait. Your attention is finite, and every interruption spends it, whether you wanted to.

Set a daily screen time limit and treat it like an appointment. Most phones now have built-in screen time controls. Set a daily limit for social media and entertainment apps, and stop when you reach it. Not tomorrow. Today. The discomfort of hitting that limit and stopping is the discipline doing its job.

Do a weekly audit. Every Sunday, look at your screen time report for the week. Not to shame yourself. To stay honest. The number will tell you whether your actions during the week matched your intentions. If they did not, adjust. That is what the audit is for.

Here is the reframe that changes everything. Your phone is not the enemy. Unconscious use of it is. Used intentionally, it is one of the most powerful tools available to a person building something. Used unconsciously, it is one of the most effective ways to spend a life without actually living it.

The hours are there. They have always been there. Take them back and watch what becomes possible when your attention finally belongs to you again.

Chapter 13

REST ISN'T WEAKNESS. SKIPPING IT IS.

This might seem like a strange chapter in a book about discipline. Sit with that tension for a moment because it is important.

Everything up to this point has been about showing up, doing the work, pushing through resistance, and refusing to let comfort make your decisions. So why is there an entire chapter about rest?

Because the driven person, the one who actually takes this book seriously and applies it, is the most likely person to run themselves into the ground and call it discipline when it is actually destruction. This chapter is specifically for you. The one who does not need to be told to work harder. The one who needs to be told that the way you are working right now is quietly costing you more than you realize.

There was a season where I was doing everything right on paper and falling apart in private. Going hard every day. Checking every box. Showing up to everything. And I was miserable. Short with my wife. Snapping at my kids. Sitting in the middle of work I claimed to care about and feeling absolutely nothing. Not tired in a way that sleep could fix. Depleted in a way that had been building for months because I had confused exhaustion with effort and busyness with progress.

That season taught me something that changed how I operate permanently. Rest is not the opposite of discipline. It expresses it. Knowing when to stop is a skill. Protecting your recovery with the same seriousness you protect your output is a discipline. And showing up fully rested and sharp is almost always more valuable than showing up exhausted and grinding.

Now let science say what it needs to say, because this is not an opinion.

Your muscles do not grow during the workout. The workout creates the stimulus. Rest is when the actual adaptation happens. Skip the recovery and you do not get stronger. You get injured or you plateau and wonder why the effort is not producing results. The same principle applies to every other area of your life.

You struggle with problem-solving when you face constraints and pressure. Research on the default mode network, the part of your brain that activates when you step away from focused work, shows that some of your most creative and insightful thinking happens during rest, walks, showers, quiet moments when you are not trying to think at all. The solution you have been grinding toward for three hours sometimes shows up five minutes after you stop and go do something else. That is not a coincidence. That is your brain doing the work it cannot do when you will not give it space.

Your relationships do not improve when you are running on empty. The version of you that shows up exhausted and stretched thin is not your best self, and the people closest to you know it, even when they do not say it. You lose your patience more quickly. Your listening gets shallower. Your presence becomes physical only. You are in the room, but you are not there. Rest gives you something left to give to the people who deserve the best of you rather than whatever is left after everything else has taken its share.

Here is what the rest is not.

Rest is not scrolling your phone for two hours because you are too tired to do anything productive. That is not a recovery. That is passive consumption that leaves your nervous system stimulated and your mind no more rested than when you started. Rest is not avoiding the hard things under the cover of needing a break. That is avoidance dressed up as self care and your body knows the difference even when your mind tries to argue otherwise.

Rest with intention is the standard. Here is what that actually looks like in practice.

Sleep is the foundation, and **it is** non-negotiable. Seven to nine hours for most adults is not a luxury. It is the biological minimum for a brain and body that are expected to perform at a high level consistently. Every hour of sleep you sacrifice in the name of productivity is an hour that quietly degrades your decision-making, your emotional regulation, your immune function, and your discipline. You cannot out discipline chronic sleep deprivation. The research on this is not ambiguous. Prioritize your sleep with the same seriousness you prioritize your most important work because without it your most important work will suffer regardless of how hard you try.

Schedule your rest the same way you schedule your work. If it is not on the calendar, it will not happen, not for the driven person. A day off means a day off. Not a day where you check email occasionally and tell yourself you are resting. Not a day where you do light work and call it recovery. An actual day off where you step away completely and let your system reset. One of those per week is not an indulgence. It is maintenance.

Learn the difference between physical rest and mental rest. Your mind can run through problems, replay conversations, and plan the next week, leaving you mentally exhausted even when sitting completely still. Physical stillness is not the same as genuine recovery. Mental rest requires disconnecting from the mental load. A walk without a podcast. Time in nature without a purpose. A meal without a screen. Activities that absorb your attention gently without demanding output. These are the things that actually restore the mental resources discipline requires.

Protect at least one thing in your week that exists purely for enjoyment. Something you do because you love it and for no other reason. That kind of rest replenishes something that output-focused recovery cannot reach. The person who has nothing in their life that exists purely for joy will eventually resent everything in their life that exists for purpose. Keep the joy. It is not a reward for finishing the work. It is what makes the work sustainable long term.

Listen to your body before it forces you to listen. Fatigue that does not resolve with a night of sleep is a warning. Persistent irritability is a warning. The inability to feel genuine enthusiasm for things you normally care about is a warning. Your body communicates clearly when it has reached its limit. The disciplined response is to hear it early and respond before it escalates into illness, injury, or burnout that costs you weeks instead of the one day of rest that could have prevented it.

The grind culture that tells you rest is weakness has produced an epidemic of burned-out, exhausted, chronically stressed people who are working incredibly hard and building very little because they never recover enough to perform at the level they are capable of. Do not let that be your story.

The people who last, the ones still standing and still sharp and still building twenty years from now, are the ones who figured out that recovery is part of the process. Not a break from the process. Part of it.

Rest on purpose. Recover with intention. And come back sharper than you left.

That is not weakness. That is how you stay in the fight long enough to win it.

PART THREE —
Discipline at Home

Chapter 14

YOUR KIDS AREN'T LISTENING TO A WORD YOU SAY — THEY'RE WATCHING EVERYTHING YOU DO

You can sit them down and explain how the world works, what it takes, why discipline matters, and why they need to take their future seriously. And they will nod. They will say okay. And then they will go do exactly what they have watched you do, not what you told them to do.

There was a season in my life where I lost almost everything. Not all at once. That is not how it usually works. It came apart slowly, the way things do when a hundred small decisions compound into a reality you did not see coming until you were already standing in the middle of it. My income, which I had built over years, vanished. The lifestyle that came with it disappeared with it. The version of life my family had grown accustomed to got smaller, quieter, and harder in ways I could feel every single day, even when I was trying not to show it.

My oldest daughter was young enough that nobody sat her down and explained what was happening. She did not know the details. She could not have understood them. But she knew. Children always know. She noticed the changes in the house before I ever said a word about them. The things that used to happen that stopped happening. Ordinary days, in their quiet moments, filled the children with tension. The way her father, who had always moved through the world as if he had everything under control, was carrying something heavy that he could not put down.

She did not ask about any of it. Instead, she made me smile. She would do extra sweet things, extra thoughtful things, telling me I was not smiling enough for her. She was a little girl trying to fix something she could not name because she loved her father and she could feel that something was wrong.

I had always been Superman in her eyes. The hardest-working man she knew. Invincible. And my biggest fear during those years was not the money, as real and relentless as that pressure was. It was that she would overhear a conversation she was not supposed to hear. That the image she had built of her father would crack. That I would fail her the way I felt I was failing everything else.

That fear was one of the most useful things I have ever felt. It reminded me that what I modeled in that house every single day was building something in my children or quietly tearing it down. I could not control how fast things turned around. But I could control what they watched me do while I was fighting to turn them around.

My oldest son gets up with me in the mornings now. He sees me going outside. He sometimes comes with me. I have never sat him down and told him to be disciplined. He just started doing what he saw me doing. That is how it works, and that is how my father did it. That is how it gets passed down.

Now, here is what this means for you practically, because understanding that your kids are watching is only the beginning. The real question is what you are giving them to watch.

Model the habits you want them to have, not the habits you are trying to overcome.

Children do not learn from your aspirations. They learn from your actions. Seeing you read is crucial for your child's reading habits, unlike hearing you declare reading's importance while you're absorbed in your phone. If you want your child to be physically active, they need to see you move your body consistently, not occasionally. If you want your child to manage money responsibly, they need to watch you make intentional financial decisions in real life, not receive a lecture about saving.

Think about the three or four habits you most want your children to carry into adulthood. Write them down if you need to. Then ask yourself honestly whether those habits are visible in your daily life right now. Not perfectly. Not without a struggle. But visibly present and consistently practiced. If they are not, the conversation about what you want for your children needs to start with a conversation about what you will do in front of them.

Ask them what they failed at today.

This is one of the most important things you can do as a parent, and almost nobody does it. Most parents ask how school was. They ask about grades, about friends, about what happened at practice. Almost nobody sits down with their child and asks what they failed at today, and means it as a compliment waiting to happen.

I ask my older kids this question regularly. Not occasionally. Regularly. And I ask it expecting an answer because I have explained to them exactly what it means. If you are not pushing your limits, you will not fail. If you never fail, you cannot grow. And growth is the game of life. Failure is not the opposite of success. It is the evidence that you are trying hard enough to actually get somewhere.

When they tell me what did not go right, the first thing I ask is how that makes them feel. I want them to sit with it honestly rather than brush past it. Then I asked, " Did you give up? " And the answer is always no. Because that is the standard in our house, and they know it. Then I ask what matters most. Did you ask for help?

That last question is the one that changes everything. Because one of the most damaging lies we accidentally teach children is that needing help is a weakness. That the goal is to figure everything out alone. That asking someone who knows more than you somehow diminishes what you accomplish. None of that is true, and all of it is crippling.

There is always someone who knows more. Someone further down the road can always shorten your learning curve, correct your form, and point out the blind spot you cannot see because you are standing too close to it. Teaching your child to seek that person out is one of the greatest gifts you can give them. And when they become the person who knows more in a particular area, teaching them to turn around and help someone else is how that gift gets passed forward.

Raise children who are not too proud to fail and not too proud to ask for help. That combination will take them further than talent, further than intelligence, and further than any advantage you could hand them.

Let them see you struggle and recover, not just succeed.

One of the most damaging things a parent can model is the appearance of effortless competence. When your children only see your wins and never see you work through difficulties, you accidentally teach them that struggle means something is wrong. That hard things are supposed to feel easy for capable people. That failure is a character flaw rather than a universal part of any meaningful effort.

Allow your children to witness you tackling hard tasks, and permit them to observe you rising early despite fatigue and fulfilling your responsibilities. Let them see you make a mistake, own it without excuses, and correct it. Let them see you ask for help when you need it. Not as a performance. Just as your normal life lived honestly in front of them.

The child who grows up watching a parent navigate difficulty with honesty and persistence becomes a grounded adult. Not one who expects the world to be easy. Not one who falls apart the first time life does not go according to plan. Not one who believes that comfort is the goal and struggle is the enemy. They become someone who knows from personal observation that hard things are survivable, that failure is temporary, and that the people who win are simply the ones who kept going.

Be consistent, not perfect.

Your children are not building an image of you from your best moments. They are building it from the pattern of your ordinary ones. The parent who is occasionally exceptional but frequently distracted, irritable, or checked out leaves a strange impression than the parent who is consistently present, consistently engaged, and consistently trying even on the hard days.

Consistency in parenting looks like this. You are available at the same times every day, not just when it is convenient. You follow through on what you say you are going to do. You enforce the same expectations today that you enforced yesterday. You bring your actual attention to the time you spend with your children rather than your physical presence and a divided mind.

None of that requires you to be a perfect parent. It requires you to be a reliable one. Reliability is what children internalize as safe. Safety allows them to develop confidence and stability, which builds discipline.

Watch what your home normalizes.

Every household has a culture. This culture sets unspoken standards for acceptability, expectations, and normalcy. Your children absorb that culture every single day. The question is whether you built it intentionally or whether it assembled itself from the path of least resistance.

It's normal in a home where screens are on from dinner through bedtime. In a home where meals happen together without phones, that is normal. It is normal in a home where adults speak to each other with impatience and frustration. In a home where conflict gets addressed directly and respectfully, that is normal. Your children will carry whatever your home normalizes into every relationship, workplace, and household they are part of for the rest of their lives.

A child raised in a home that expects effort, examines failure instead of hiding it, encourages seeking help without shame, and normalizes hard work will not grow up believing money appears without sacrifice or success arrives without struggle. That groundedness is rare. People build it at home, in the ordinary texture of daily life, long before the world has time to teach them its harder lessons.

You have more influence over who your children become than any school, any coach, any friend group, or any algorithm. That influence does not come from what you tell them. It comes from what you show them, every ordinary day, in the way you live your life inside your own house.

You do not have to be perfect. Be present. Be consistent. And you have to be honest enough with yourself to model the things you actually want passed down rather than the things you are still trying to overcome.

They are watching. Make it worth seeing.

Chapter 15

A Great Marriage Doesn't Just Happen. It Gets Built Every Single Day.

I need to tell you something about my wife.

She would not have given the old me five minutes. Not because she is harsh or judgmental. Because she is exceptional. She is the smartest person I have ever met. And exceptional people do not settle for potential. They respond to who you actually are.

The man I was before discipline, the one making airtight excuses, sleeping on his ambition, driving a nice car he could barely afford, running from every hard thing that required more than effort to solve, that man never walks a woman like her down the aisle. Never. The life I have now, the marriage I have now, was not available to the old version of me. I had to become someone worth choosing before someone worth choosing would choose me.

I rank her second only to God. My wife is the teammate who makes everything else possible. Four kids, a business, a YouTube channel, a book— none of it works without someone in your corner who believes in what you are building and holds things together when you are in the middle of building it. When I say I could do none of this without her, I am not being poetic. I am being precise.

Discipline did not just change my habits. It changed what my life could be. And nowhere is that more true than in my marriage.

Here is what nobody tells you about marriage when you are standing at the altar, full of intention and feeling. The ceremony is one day long. The marriage is every day after it. And every day thereafter it requires a decision. Not a feeling. Not an inspiration. A decision. To show up, engage, and choose the person you committed to, even on the days when choosing them is inconvenient, uncomfortable, or the last thing you feel like doing.

That is not a romantic idea. It is the most practical truth about long-term partnerships that exists. And most marriages do not fail because of one catastrophic moment. They fail because of a thousand small moments where someone chose something else, the phone, the silence, the easier path, over the person sitting right next to them. Those moments stack up quietly over months and years until two people who once chose each other every day wake up feeling like strangers who share a house.

Discipline in marriage is the antidote. Here is what it actually looks like.

Have the conversation you have been avoiding.

There is something in your marriage right now that needs to be said and has not been. You know what it is. You have been carrying it around, telling yourself the timing is not right, that it will start a fight, that things are fine enough and it is not worth the disruption.

It is worth the disruption. The things left unsaid in a marriage do not disappear. They calcify. A distance develops between them that neither person can quite explain. They become the resentment that shows up sideways in arguments about things that do not actually matter. The conversation you are avoiding today is the problem that will be three times harder to address six months from now.

This is true regardless of who you are or what role you play in your household. The wife who has been suppressing her frustration for months. The husband who has been sidestepping financial discussions. The partner who feels invisible and has not communicated this. The one who knows something is off but keeps hoping it resolves itself. It will not resolve itself. It needs a voice.

Disciplined couples have hard conversations early and often. Not because they enjoy conflict. Because they respect the relationship enough to keep it clean. Saying the hard thing when it is still manageable is an act of love, even when it does not feel like one in the moment.

Put the phone down.

This is small, and it is enormous at the same time. When your spouse is talking to you, put the phone face down and look at them. Not because they asked you to. Because they matter more than whatever is on the screen. Because the message that is sent, repeated daily over years, is that you are present, that they have your attention, that they are worth more than a notification.

The opposite message, delivered just as clearly and just as consistently, is that they are competing with a device for your attention and losing. People feel that. They may not bring it up. They may tell themselves it is not a big deal. But it registers. Every time. And over the years it builds into something that is very much a big deal.

Full presence is one of the most valuable things you can offer another person. In a world engineered to divide your attention into smaller and smaller pieces, choosing to give someone all of it, even for fifteen minutes, is increasingly rare and increasingly meaningful. Every person in a marriage deserves that. Make sure yours is getting it.

Apologize without conditions.

A genuine apology has no second half. The sentence does not end with the word 'but'. They did not provide you with an explanation for your justification. It does not arrive only after the other person has also acknowledged their part. It stands alone.

Pride is one of the most expensive things anyone can carry into a marriage. It costs more than almost any argument is worth, and it collects interest. The discipline to say I was wrong, I am sorry, without immediately defending yourself or redirecting blame, is one of the most powerful things you can bring to a partnership. It has a way of disarming people. It repairs. If you realize it , it models something your children are watching and absorbing.

This is not about one partner always apologizing and the other never having to. It is about both people being willing to go first. Being willing to value the relationship over the need to win. That willingness, practiced consistently by both people, changes the entire culture of a marriage.

Apologizing when your pride does not want to is not weakness. It is the decision that the relationship matters more than being right. Make that decision quickly and make it often.

Do the small things without being asked.

Great marriages do not rely on grand gestures. They build great marriages through the consistent repetition of slight gestures, which then form the relationship's language. He made the cup of coffee without asking. You handled the errand because you knew it would lighten their load. The question asked that says I am paying attention to your life, not just living alongside it.

These things take almost no time. They require almost no effort. And they communicate something that no anniversary trip or expensive gift can replicate, which is that your partner is on your mind when there is no occasion requiring it. That you notice them. That they are not furniture in the story of your life, but the reason the story is worth telling.

Every person expresses and receives love differently. What feels like care to you may not land the same way for your spouse. Pay attention to what your partner actually responds to, not what you think they should appreciate. Then do that thing, consistently, without waiting to be asked and without expecting acknowledgment every time. That is the discipline. That is what separates the couples who drift from the couples who deepen.

Carry your weight and then some.

A marriage where one person is quietly carrying more than their share while the other remains unaware is a marriage building toward resentment. It does not matter who earns more, who works outside the home, or what the division of responsibilities looks like on paper. What matters is that both people are paying attention to what needs to be done and doing it without the other person having to manage them like an employee.

Look around your household and ask yourself honestly whether your partner is carrying something you could help with. The mental load of managing a family, remembering appointments, anticipating needs, tracking what is running low, planning what comes next, is real, and it is exhausting. It often falls disproportionately on one person while the other moves through the house unaware of how much invisible work is holding everything together.

Take the initiative before someone asks you to. Notice what your partner is managing and take something off their plate. Do it today and do it again tomorrow. That kind of attentiveness is not just helpful. It is one of the most intimate things you can do for someone you share a life with.

Protect your marriage from neglect.

Neglect is the most common way good marriages end and the least dramatic. Nobody chooses it deliberately. It accumulates in the gaps between busy seasons, in the years when the kids are young and the work is demanding and the marriage gets treated like a thing that can wait because it seems stable. It can wait. Until it cannot.

Schedule time with your spouse the same way you schedule everything else that matters to you. A weekly date does not have to be expensive or elaborate. It has to be consistent, and it has to be protected. No rescheduling because something else came up. Your marriage is no less important than the thing that came up. Treat it accordingly.

Check in with your partner regularly in a way that goes beyond logistics. Not just who is picking up the kids and what is for dinner. Find out how they are truly doing. Ask what they need from you this week. Ask what they carry; you might help with it. Those questions keep two people connected through the ordinary seasons that would otherwise quietly pull them apart.

Become the person your marriage needs, not just the person you want to be.

Every person brings something into a marriage that their partner did not ask for and did not sign up for. Old wounds. Bad habits. Blind spots. Tendencies that made sense in an earlier version of your life and cause damage in this one. The disciplined partner looks honestly at their contributions and undertakes the work to address them, rather than expecting their spouse to absorb it indefinitely.

Personal growth is not just a solo project. In a marriage, they share it. The work you do on yourself directly affects the person living closest to you. Becoming more patient, more present, more honest, more emotionally available, these are not just gifts to yourself. They are gifts to your marriage and to every person in your household.

This applies to both partners equally. The husband who struggles to control his temper or the wife who resists confronting her avoidance. The partner who knows they need help to process something old and keeps putting it off. Growth is not optional in a marriage that lasts. It is the ongoing cost of building something worth having.

The marriage you want is available to you. But we build it every single day out of the decisions most people consider too small to matter. They are not too small. They are everything.

Choose your partner today. And then choose them again tomorrow.

Chapter 16

WHO ARE YOU WHEN NOBODY'S WATCHING? THAT'S YOUR REAL ANSWER.

Here is where you find out who you really are. Not when there are people watching or when you are being held accountable. Not when someone is going to check your work. When nobody knows. When nobody will ever find out whether you did it. That is where discipline lives or dies.

Anyone can discipline themselves when an audience is present. When your boss is watching, or when your trainer is counting reps. When you post your workout on social media. That is performance, not discipline. Performance requires a stage. Discipline requires nothing but your own decision.

There was a season in my life when I was alone with a reality long before anyone else knew it was happening. No audience. No one was watching to see if I would hold it together or fall apart. Just me, the weight of what was happening, and the choice of who I was going to be in the dark.

My father said something to me during that time that I have never forgotten. He told me that storms sometimes last a long time, but they always end. Then he said something that shifted the way I saw everything. Some people plant during storms because they see it as free rain. Others only see the storm.

That hit me as a gardener. Because I had a choice about which person I was going to be. Nobody was going to give me credit for choosing right. Nobody was watching. But I made a decision that during that storm I was going to plant.

So every night when the house was quiet and nobody could see me, I did something Socrates pointed me toward long before I understood why. He wrote that an unexamined life is not worth living. So I examined mine. Every night I audited my decisions. Where I had gone wrong.

What I could have done differently. What I was going to do tomorrow. Not to punish myself, but to understand myself. To make sure the man going to sleep was clearer than the man who woke up that morning.

And every morning I had a schedule. A plan. And I executed that plan. Nobody was checking. Nobody would have known if I had skipped it. But I knew. And that was enough.

Now, here is what this means for you. Because private discipline is not just a concept worth admiring. It is a practice worth building. And it looks like specific things done consistently when no one is watching.

Your private decisions are your actual character.

The version of you that exists when there is no audience is the truest version of you. Not the one you perform for your boss, or your followers, or your family at Sunday dinner. The one who decides what to do at 10 PM when the day is over and nobody is paying attention. When no meal plan is available, they decide what to eat. The one who either does the work or finds a reason not to when there is no one to answer to but yourself.

That version of you is building something, whether you are aware of it or not. Every private decision is a vote for the person you are becoming. Skip the workout when nobody is watching, and you teach yourself that your commitments are negotiable. Follow through when nobody is watching, and you teach yourself that your word means something regardless of who is in the room.

The person who cuts corners in private eventually cuts corners in public. It leaks. It always leaks. The shortcuts become habits. The habits become character. And the character does not stay hidden. It surfaces in how you handle pressure, how you treat people when you are tired, how you respond when things go wrong and nobody is around to see you do it.

But it works both ways. Your private discipline influences everything you do. Your confidence goes up because you know you are not faking it. You walk into rooms differently when you are not carrying the weight of private corners you have been cutting. Your integrity is intact because you are not performing for an audience. You are simply being who you are, regardless of who is watching.

Remove decisions that drain your energy for no reason.

Every decision you make costs something. Not money. Mental energy. And mental energy spent on decisions that do not matter is mental energy unavailable for decisions that do. So structure and systems are not just organizational tools. They are discipline tools. They protect your capacity for the things that actually require your full attention.

Every video I have ever made for my YouTube channel, I am wearing all black. Not because it looks good on camera. Not because it is a brand choice. Because it is a reminder. A reminder of why I started. A reminder to stay disciplined and show up even when I do not feel like recording. And practically, wearing all black means I never have to think about what to wear. I removed that decision entirely. I show up; I am in black, and my mind is free to focus on what actually matters, which is helping the person on the other side of the screen.

Look at your own life and identify the small, recurring decisions that cost you energy, producing nothing meaningful. The clothes you choose to wear. Your breakfast choices. What time do you work out? What order do you start morning tasks? Systematize as many of those as you reasonably can. Not because the decisions are unimportant, but because the energy they consume is better used elsewhere. The goal is not to eliminate choice from your life. The goal is to reserve your sharpest thinking for the choices that actually shape where you are going.

Discipline is not just about the big decisions. It is about removing the small, unnecessary ones so your energy goes where it counts.

Do the private work of honest self-examination.

Here is something nobody tells you about the areas of life where people struggle most. The problem is rarely a lack of information or effort. It is a lack of honest self-assessment. People work hard in the wrong direction for years because they never stop long enough to examine whether what they are doing is actually working. They avoid the honest look because the honest look is uncomfortable and there is no one forcing them to take it.

Private discipline requires you to be your own most honest observer. Not your harshest critic. Your most honest one. There is a difference. The harsh critic tears down without direction. The honest observer looks clearly at what is happening, names it accurately, and asks what needs to change.

This means sitting alone with your decisions regularly and asking real questions. Not the comfortable ones. The ones that actually reveal something. Did I do what I said I was going to do today? Where did I cut a corner I did not need to cut? What am I avoiding right now and why? What would the best version of me have done differently today?

Those questions are uncomfortable. That discomfort is the point. Growth does not happen in the absence of honest feedback. And when no one else is providing that feedback, you have to provide it for yourself. The people who improve consistently are not the ones with the best coaches or the best circumstances. They are the ones who have learned to tell themselves the truth in private.

Plant in the storm.

Whatever difficult season you are in right now, there is something you can build inside it. Something that will matter when the storm passes. A skill, a habit, a relationship. A practice. The people who come out of hard times better than they went in are not the ones who had it easier. They are the ones who refused to let the difficulty go to waste.

You do not get credit for planting in the storm. Nobody sees it happening. Nobody applauds it. The sun will reveal the results later, and by then, most people will only see what grew, not the conditions it grew in. That is fine. That is exactly the point. Private discipline does not need an audience. It needs your commitment.

Plant anyway. Show up anyway. Do the work in the dark and trust that what you build in private will stand in public.

The Nightly Audit

Three questions. Write them somewhere you will see them every night.

1. What decision did I make today that I need to own?

2. What did I avoid today that I need to face tomorrow?

3. Does the person who goes to sleep tonight represent who I am trying to become?

Answer them honestly. Five minutes. Every night.

It will change you.

Chapter 17

Stop Lecturing Your Kids. Build the System That Does It For You.

If you have kids, you have tried the lecture. You sit them down, explain why something matters, lay out the consequences, and hope it sticks. About ninety percent of the time, it does not. Their eyes glaze over. They say okay. And then they go right back to whatever they were doing before you opened your mouth.

Here is the hard truth about lectures. They feel productive because you are talking and they are nodding. But nodding is not learning. Nodding is waiting for you to finish. If you want your children to develop discipline, stop trying to talk them into it and start building an environment that produces it naturally. You build that environment with structure, consistency, and expectations that you enforce without negotiation every single time.

This is not about being a drill sergeant. It is about being an architect. Your job is to design a home where disciplined behavior simply happens, not because your kids feel inspired by your speeches but because the structure of their daily life requires it of them.

Here is how to build that.

Start with who your family is, not just what they do.

Years ago, I worked at The Ritz-Carlton. They required me to learn the Ritz-Carlton Credo word for word. Not skim it. Not be familiar with it. Know it. Recite it. Live it on the floor every single shift. The Credo was not a suggestion. The Credo served as the standard for every employee, irrespective of their role, mood, or daily experiences.

I remember standing there, thinking, this is remarkable. The company took the time to define its identity, values, and the expectations for its representatives. And they required every employee to internalize it completely.

Then it hit me. I was learning a company's creed word for word. I was required to know it and live it at work. But I had created nothing like that for my family.

So I did.

Our family now has a creed. A written declaration of who we are, what we stand for, what we bring to the world, and what it means to be a member of this family. My children know it. We revisit it. It is not hanging on a wall collecting dust. It is a standard of living that shapes how we carry ourselves individually and together.

Think about that for a moment. We memorize company mottos. We recite pledges to organizations. We learn the values of employers and sports teams, and schools. How many families have actually sat down and defined their own? How many households operate for decades without ever putting into words what they are actually about?

Your family is the most important organization you will ever be part of. It deserves a creed.

Creating one does not have to be complicated. Sit down with your family and ask three questions. What kind of people do we want to be? How do we want to treat each other and the world? What do we want people to say about our family? The answers to those questions, shaped into an abrupt declaration that everyone agrees on and everyone can recite, become the standard your household operates. Not rules imposed from the top down. A shared identity that everyone has ownership over because everyone helped build it.

When your child is about to make a poor decision and you can say does that represent who our family is, you are no longer the authority figure handing down a judgment. You are holding them to a standard they agreed to. That is a completely different conversation, and it lands completely differently.

Start with a small set of non-negotiable daily expectations.

The mistake most parents make is trying to install too much structure at once. They see a problem and respond with a list of new rules that collapses under its own weight within a week because nobody, including the parent, can keep track of all of it. Start smaller than you think you need to.

Pick three to five daily expectations that are simple, visible, and completable without supervision. Make the bed every morning. Put the dishes in the sink or dishwasher after every meal. Homework before any screens. Clothes off the floor before bed. These are not big asks. They are small enough to be done in minutes and significant enough to matter.

The goal of these expectations is not the task itself. It is the habit of compliance with a standard. A child who makes their bed every morning without being reminded is not just learning to make a bed. They learn that there are things in life that get done regardless of how they feel about it that morning. That lesson will serve them in every job, every relationship, and every hard season they encounter for the rest of their lives.

Consistency is the entire game.

You can have the best set of household expectations in the world, and they will mean nothing if you enforce them only when you feel like it. The moment you let something slide because you are tired, or distracted, or it does not seem worth the battle tonight, you have taught your child something more powerful than any rule you have ever set. You have taught them that the standard is negotiable.

Kids are not testing you to be difficult. They are testing you because testing is how they figure out where the real boundaries are. Every time you hold the line, you confirm the boundary is real. Every time you let it go, you confirm the boundary is a suggestion. They will act accordingly either way.

Enforcement does not have to be loud or dramatic. It just has to be consistent. A calm, firm reminder followed by a consequence that actually happens is more effective than ten angry lectures followed by nothing. The emotion is not what teaches them. The consistency is.

When you are consistent, your children stop testing as frequently because they already know the answer. The battle gets shorter over time, not longer. But you have to hold the line long enough to get there.

Build routines that run on autopilot.

A routine is a sequence of behaviors that happens in the same order at the same time consistently enough that it eventually requires no decision making at all. It just runs. This is exactly what you want for your children because it removes the daily negotiation entirely.

A morning routine practiced the same way every school day becomes automatic within a few weeks. Wake up, make the bed, get dressed, eat breakfast, backpack by the door. They are not deciding whether to do these things. They are just doing them. The routine carries the weight so you do not have to.

Build an after-school routine with the same intentionality. Backpack down, snack, homework, then free time. In that order every day. Not homework when they feel like it. Not homework after two hours of screens. Homework first, every time, and then the screen time they have earned. Sequence matters. When the reward consistently follows the responsibility, children stop arguing about whether to do the responsibility. They just do it to get to the other side.

An evening routine anchors the end of the day in the same way. Dishes away, shower, clothes out for tomorrow, thirty minutes of reading or quiet time, lights out. When the evening has a predictable shape, children wind down more easily, sleep better, and wake up less chaotically. The routine is doing the parenting for you.

Match the consequence to the behavior and deliver it every time.

Consequences only work when they are predictable and consistent. A consequence your child is not sure will actually happen is not a consequence. It is a bluff. And children call bluffs with remarkable precision.

The consequence does not have to be severe to be effective. It has to be certain. If you don't do your homework before screen time, you won't have screens that evening, period, without exception or lengthy discussion. If the bed is not made, there is a consequence that happens immediately and without drama. The less emotional energy you put into enforcing the consequence, the more effective it is. You are not angry or disappointed. You are simply following through on exactly what you said would happen. That calm predictability builds respect for the standard.

Avoid the warning spiral. One warning is reasonable. Two warnings teach your child that they have at least two chances before anything really happens. Three warnings tell them the consequence is not coming for a while yet. Give the instruction once, give one simple reminder, and then follow through. That sequence, practiced consistently, produces a child who takes the first instruction seriously rather than waiting to see how many times you will ask.

Adjust the system as they grow, not the standard.

Expectations for a seven-year-old differ from those suitable for a twelve-year-old or a sixteen-year-old. The standard that they are responsible, consistent, and follow through on their commitments never changes. How we apply the standard evolves as they do.

As your children get older, give them more ownership over how their responsibilities get done while holding firm on whether they get done. A teenager does not need you to design their morning routine minute by minute. They need you to expect them to be ready on time, maintain their space, and keep their commitments. How they get there is increasingly up to them. That shift from you managing the process to them managing it, with you holding the standard, is how you raise a child who eventually manages themselves as an adult.

The goal of all of this is not a perfectly obedient child. It is an adult who does not need to be managed. Punctuality is a characteristic of those who arrive on time. Who follows through because their word means something to them. Who does the hard thing without being told because their upbringing instilled in them that the hard thing was simply what people did.

We memorize the creeds of companies. We learn the mottos of organizations that employ us for a few years and move on. Your family is the organization that lasts a lifetime. Give it a standard worth living up to.

Write the creed. Build the routines. Hold the standard. And let the daily texture of your household do the teaching that no lecture ever could.

Chapter 18

YOUR HOME IS CHAOTIC BECAUSE YOU'RE RELYING ON WILLPOWER INSTEAD OF THIS

If your household depends on everyone remembering to do things, it is going to fall apart. Not sometimes. Consistently. Because memory is unreliable, willpower runs out, and motivation comes and goes like the weather. You cannot build a stable home on resources that fluctuate daily. You build it on systems that run regardless of how anyone feels on a given Tuesday morning.

A system is any structure that removes the need for constant decision-making. It takes a recurring situation and gives it a permanent answer so that the answer never has to be negotiated again. Trash goes out on Wednesday night. That is the system. Nobody has to remember, nobody has to ask, nobody has to be reminded. Wednesday night, the trash goes out. They made the decision once, and now it just runs.

That is what a well-run household feels like from the inside. Not rigid. Not military. Just clear. Everybody knows their role. Everybody knows the order. Things get done without arguments, without reminders, and without one person silently carrying the mental load for everyone else while quietly resenting it.

During the most difficult financial period of my life, I finally understood the true cost of lacking systems. I had been operating on effort and willpower for years, in every area of my life, and when the pressure got heavy enough, both of them gave out. The chaos that followed was not just external. It was internal. Nothing had structure. Nothing ran on its own. Everything required my constant attention and energy; I no longer had any . That season showed me that systems are not a luxury for people with simple lives. They are a necessity for anyone trying to hold something together under pressure.

Here is how to build them across the areas of your home that matter most.

The Morning System

Chaotic mornings almost always result from people pushing decisions, which they should have made the night before, to the worst possible time, when everyone is tired, rushed, and operating on no caffeine. The fix is a simple evening prep routine that loads the next morning before it starts.

Clothes laid out the night before. Backpacks packed and by the door. Lunches made or planned. A consistent wake-up time that does not change based on how late everyone stayed up. These adjustments are not complicated. Together they eliminate the four or five minor crises that turn a morning into a scramble and send everyone out the door already behind.

The morning itself should have a sequence that everyone in the household knows and follows in the same order every day. Not a rigid minute by minute schedule. A sequence. Wake up , make the bed, get dressed, eat, handle hygiene, out the door. When the sequence is consistent, it becomes automatic. Automatic means no arguments, no reminders, no one person herding everyone else while their own morning falls apart.

The Household Responsibility System

One of the fastest ways to create resentment in a home is to leave responsibilities undefined. When nobody knows whose job something is, it either falls on the most responsible person every time, or it does not get done and becomes a source of tension. Neither outcome is sustainable.

Sit down with your household and define who owns what. Not informally. Actually, write it down. Cooking, dishes, laundry, groceries, trash, lawn, finances, school pickups, whatever the recurring responsibilities are in your home, every one of them needs a clear owner. Not a person who does it when they get around to it. A person who owns it and is accountable for it getting done.

For households with children, age-appropriate responsibilities are not optional extras. They are part of raising functioning adults. A six-year-old can clean their plate and make their bed. A ten-year-old can manage their laundry and help with dinner. A teenager can fully manage several household responsibilities. Giving children real ownership over tasks teaches them that the household runs because everyone contributes, not because one or two adults handle everything invisibly in the background.

Defining and owning responsibilities distributes the mental load. Burnout is no longer an issue for the person who has been discreetly managing everything. The people who have been passively benefiting start contributing. The home runs better, and the relationships within the home carry less unspoken weight.

The Weekly Reset

Every well-run household needs a weekly moment where the coming week gets organized before it arrives. Sunday works for most families, but the day matters less than the consistency. Pick one time per week when the household briefly syncs.

What does the week look like? Who has what commitments on which days? What meals are being cooked and what needs to be at the grocery store to make that happen? Which bills need to be paid? What appointments need to be kept? What did not get done last week that needs to carry forward?

This does not have to be a long meeting. Fifteen to twenty minutes. But those fifteen minutes prevent the mid-week scramble where nobody knows who is picking up which kid, there is nothing in the refrigerator, and a bill got missed because nobody was tracking it. The weekly reset is the system that keeps all the other systems coordinated.

The Financial System

Money chaos in a household is almost always a systems problem disguised as an income problem. Most households do not fail financially because they do not earn enough. They fail because there is no structure governing where the money goes once it arrives.

Build a simple system with three components. First, every dollar that comes in has a destination before anyone spends it. Fixed expenses, savings, and discretionary spending are all allocated in advance, not figured out after the fact when the account is already lower than expected. Second, one person reviews the accounts every week, not monthly. Weekly visibility catches problems while they are still small. Monthly reviews find problems after the damage has already been done. Third, one shared financial goal is always active. An emergency fund. A vacation. A home repair. Debt being paid off. Shared goals give both partners a reason to make the same disciplined decisions rather than pulling in different directions.

The financial system does not require a complicated spreadsheet or expensive software. It requires straightforward answers to three questions. What is coming in? Where is it going? And are we on track toward what we agreed matters most? When both people in a household can answer those three questions without hesitation, the financial arguments drop dramatically because the system has already decided.

The Communication System

Most household tension is not really about the thing it appears to be about. It is about unmet expectations that were never clearly communicated and unresolved issues that got buried under the busyness of daily life until they surfaced as an argument about something unrelated.

Build a simple communication system that keeps the household connected before things escalate. A brief daily check-in between partners, even five minutes, maintains the connection that gets lost when two people are managing a household and a family and running in different directions all week. A weekly conversation that goes beyond logistics, one that asks How are you actually doing? What do you need? What are you carrying right now that keeps minor issues from becoming major ones?

With children, a brief daily touchpoint, dinner together, a few minutes before bed, a question asked and genuinely listened to— keeps the relationship current. Kids do not bring things up on your schedule. They bring them up when they feel connected enough to talk. The system that keeps you consistently present and available is what creates those moments.

Systems do not remove humanity from a home. They protect it. When the logistics run on their own, the people inside the home have more energy for each other. Less friction over who forgot what. Less resentment over who is carrying more. Less chaos bleeding into the hours that should belong to the people you love most.

The most disciplined households are not the ones where everyone is trying the hardest. They are the ones where the structure does the heavy lifting so the people inside it do not have to.

Build the system once. Let it run. And use the energy you save for the things that actually matter.

PART FOUR — DISCIPLINE IN WORK AND MONEY

Chapter 19

The Days You Don't Feel Like It Are the Days That Actually Count

There will be days when you do not feel like doing anything. The work is boring. The progress is invisible. Nobody is noticing. Nothing exciting is happening. Every part of you wants to coast, to reschedule, to give yourself permission to pick it back up tomorrow when you might feel more like it.

Show up anyway.

After losing everything I had built, I took a job as a sales director at a gym chain. I felt defeated. This was a good job, but I had owned something of my own. I had built something from nothing, poured years into it, and now I was working for someone else in an industry I had just failed to build on my own, doing a job that had nothing to do with the future I was trying to build. I hated every second of it in the beginning.

But after months of honest conversations with my mentor, after reading the books he pushed me toward, after sitting alone at night with a journal and telling myself the truth about where I was and why, something shifted. I stopped seeing that job as a punishment and started seeing it as a stepping stone. And the moment that shift happened, I changed how I showed up. Early every morning. Late every evening. Working as if my last name were on the building. Not because I loved the work. Because I had decided that wherever I was, I was going to be someone who showed up fully, regardless of how I felt about being there.

Wherever I was on God's green planet, I vowed to myself I would give my all.

That job became the savings account that eventually allowed me to move to Florida, the state where my life had cracked open years before, and start building again. The breakthrough came from the stepping stone. And the stepping stone only worked because I showed up to it on the days I did not want to.

That is the lesson. And here is what it means for you practically. **Understand what is actually happening on the hard days.**

The days you do not feel like showing up are not signs that something is wrong. They are not signals that you are on the wrong path, or that the work does not matter, or that you need a change. They are a completely normal and predictable part of any meaningful pursuit. Every person who has ever built something worth having has sat exactly where you are sitting right now, staring at the work, feeling nothing, wondering why it does not feel the way they thought it would feel.

The excitement you felt when you started was real. It was also temporary. Excitement is the emotion of beginning. Excitement does not last. What lasts is the decision you made when you started, the reason behind the work, the person you committed to becoming. When the excitement leaves, those things remain. The question is whether you built your practice on excitement or on the decision.

If you build it on excitement, you will stop when the excitement stops. If you build it on the decision, you will keep going because the decision does not change based on how you feel in the morning. Decide once, clearly and seriously, and then let that decision carry you through every day the feeling refuses to.

Lower the bar on hard days, not the standard.

One of the most practical things you can do on the days you do not feel like showing up is to reduce what showing up requires rather than eliminating it entirely. The standard that you showed up, never changes. You can adjust what counts as showing up based on what the day will realistically bear.

On your best days, you can bring everything. Full effort, full focus, full output. On your hardest days, you bring something. Not nothing. Something. Despite being half the normal length, they completed the workout. The chapter that is three paragraphs instead of three pages still got written. The calls that were made even though you were not feeling sharp still moved the needle. Something is always better than nothing because something maintains the habit and nothing breaks it.

The person who shows up at fifty percent on their hard days will always outperform the person who waits until they feel one hundred percent before they start. Because one hundred percent days are rarer than anyone admits. And the habit of waiting for them is just the habit of not showing up dressed up in higher standards.

Change your environment before you quit.

Switching your work environment might help you decide you can work today. Before you decide you cannot work out today, change where you are working out. Before you decide you have nothing to say today, change what you are doing for the next twenty minutes and come back.

The environment has a powerful effect on a mental state that most people dramatically underestimate. When someone struggles to think clearly at their desk, they often find ideas flow after a twenty-minute walk. The same person who cannot find motivation in their home gym sometimes shows up completely differently at a different location. The problem on those days is often not the work. It is the environment that has become associated with resistance.

When you feel resistance coming, move before you negotiate with it. Go outside. Change rooms. Drive somewhere different. Put on something that signals to your brain that work is happening. Small environmental shifts can break the mental state that is keeping you stuck faster than any motivational content you could consume.

Reconnect with your reason, not your feeling.

On the days that feeling is gone, your reason is the only thing that can replace it. Why does this work matter? Who is it for? What does the version of your life that you are building actually look like, and how does what you are avoiding today connect to getting there or not getting there?

This is not a motivational exercise. It is practical. Your reason is the anchor that holds when everything else is drifting. But it only works if you know it clearly enough to return to it when you need it. Vague reasons produce vague commitment. Specific reasons produce specific resilience.

Write why you are doing the work you are doing. Not a general answer. A specific one. Who depends on it? What makes it possible?

What it means about who you are becoming. Keep it somewhere you can see it on the days your feelings tell you it does not matter. Your feelings are unreliable narrators. Your reason is not valid .

Remember that dry seasons set up breakthroughs.

Looking back at every area of my life where something real eventually happened, the season just before the breakthrough almost always felt like nothing was moving. The content that no one was watching. The fitness routine that seemed to be just about maintenance. Slowly building a cushion, the financial habits were barely noticeable. Nothing felt significant. Nothing felt as if it was working.

And then something shifted. Not because of one dramatic moment, but because of everything that had been accumulating quietly in the background during all those ordinary days when I showed up and nothing seemed to happen.

That is how it works. The compound effect does not announce itself while it is building. It is silent and invisible right until it is not. The breakthrough looks sudden from the outside. From the inside, it is just the day the work finally became visible. The work itself started on all those days that felt like they did not matter.

They all mattered. Every single one of them.

You do not get to choose when the results show up. You only get to choose whether you are still working when they do. So show up today. Do the boring work. Put in the invisible effort. Trust the process when the process gives you nothing back.

The days you do not feel like it are not the obstacle. They are the works. And they are the days that separate the people who eventually get somewhere from the people who are still talking about getting there.

Show up. Especially when you do not feel like it. That is when it counts the most.

Chapter 20

DISTRACTIONS DON'T INTERRUPT YOUR FOCUS. THEY EAT IT ALIVE.

Distractions are the silent killers of discipline. They do not feel dangerous because they are small. A quick scroll here. A notification there. A conversation that pulls you off track for twenty minutes. Individually, none of them seem like a big deal. Collectively, they eat your day alive.

The science on this is not subtle. Research shows it takes over twenty minutes to return to the same level of concentration after an interruption. That two-minute text message did not cost you two minutes. It cost you twenty-two. And if that happens several times an hour, you are not really working. You are sitting near work, doing a convincing impression of a productive person while your actual output quietly bleeds out through every crack in your focus.

But here is what nobody talks about when they discuss distraction. The most dangerous ones are not on your phone. They are not in your environment. They are inside you. And they do not look like distractions at all. What they resemble appears to be personality. They look like preferences. They look like just who you are.

I am a private person by nature. Always have been. My oldest daughter used to say I reminded her of Ron Swanson from Parks and Recreation. If you know that character, you will understand exactly what she meant. Quiet. Self-contained. The world kept small, and the circle kept smaller.

For years I poured into people constantly through mastermind groups I had built with over fifty men, through friends of friends who needed guidance, through neighbors who heard about me through word of mouth. Real impact. Real lives changed. I just was not doing any of it publicly. And I told myself that was fine. That private impact was enough.

Then it was not. Not because I was doing something wrong, but because the reach was too small for what I had put into myself. I should not hoard the knowledge I had accumulated over 20 years of gardening, fitness, health, and mental toughness within a mastermind group or disseminate it solely through neighbor recommendations. It went further.

I did not want to do it. Filming videos is not natural to me. Writing this honestly for strangers to read is not natural to me. Everything I am doing now, the YouTube channel, the podcast, this book, exists outside of my natural comfort zone. Every single piece of it required me to walk directly into what felt most unnatural and do it, anyway.

The distraction I had to eliminate was not a bad habit. It was my privacy. My comfort with staying small. My preference for helping people I could see and know rather than putting myself in front of a camera for people I would never meet. That comfort was a distraction. Respectable, easy to defend, and standing directly between me and what I was supposed to be doing with my life.

I showed up anyway. I helped the few when the numbers were small. I kept going when the audience was tiny and the effort felt completely disproportionate to the results. That consistency eventually became GrowFitFL. Thousands of people have had their lives touched by content I almost never created because I was too comfortable being private to be useful.

Now, here is what this means for you. Because you have both kinds of distractions in your life, and both of them are costing you more than you realize.

Eliminate the external distractions first because they are the easiest to fix.

Your phone is the most obvious one, and it has its own chapter in this book. But the phone is one item on a longer list. Distractions arise from every open browser tab unrelated to your current task. Every notification that interrupts a focused block of work is a distraction. Any individual who captures your attention while you're engaged in deep work makes up a distraction. Every noisy, visually cluttered, uncomfortable environment that makes sustained focus harder than it needs to be is a distraction.

The fix for external distractions is environmental design. You are not trying to resist them through willpower. You are removing them from the environment so the willpower question never comes up. Phone in another room during focused work, not face down on the desk, in another room. Browser tabs closed except the one you need. Notifications off for everything that does not require an immediate response. A workspace that signals to your brain that work happens here. Close the door or headphones on headphones as a signal to others that you are unavailable.

Protect your focused time blocks as if they are the most valuable things you own. Because they are. Every hour of genuine, uninterrupted focus produces over three hours of distracted half-presence. Fewer proper hours of work consistently outperform more hours of fragmented attention. Design your environment for focus and stop relying on willpower to find it inside a space engineered against it.

Then do the harder work of examining the internal ones.

External distractions are inconvenient. Internal distractions are identity-level. They are the ones that look like who you are rather than what you are doing wrong, which is exactly what makes them so difficult to see and so costly to ignore.

Internal distractions take different forms for different people. The comfort of remaining private, of housing work, gifts, and knowledge within a small, trusted circle where it feels safe and manageable appeals to some. For others, it is perfectionism, the refusal to ship the work, share the idea, or start the project until it is ready, and it is never quite ready. For others, it is the pull toward what is familiar over what is necessary, the gravitational force of the life they have always lived making the life they are supposed to be building feel like a threat rather than a destination.

None of these feel like distractions from the inside. They feel like reasonable caution. Like wisdom. Like knowing yourself. And sometimes they are. But sometimes the thing you are calling self-awareness is actually self-protection. You actively shield yourself, limiting your existence to a scope smaller than your intended capacity.

Ask yourself honestly what you are not doing that you know you should be doing. Not the tasks on your to-do list. The bigger things.

That job you continuously postpone starting. The version of yourself you keep describing in the future tense without moving toward in the present tense. The contribution you know you make, you keep finding sophisticated reasons to delay.

That thing you are circling is where your real distraction lives. And unlike a phone notification, it will not announce itself. It will just quietly consume the years while you stay busy with everything except the thing that matters most.

Build a distraction audit into your week.

Once a week, ideally during your weekly reset, spend ten minutes asking yourself two questions. What interrupted my focus this week that I could have controlled? And what am I avoiding this week that I am dressing up as something else?

The first question catches external distractions. The second catches the internal ones. Together they give you an honest picture of where your attention actually went versus where you intended it to go. Over time, this audit becomes one of the most valuable discipline tools you have because it keeps you honest about the gap between your intentions and your actions before that gap becomes a canyon.

Write the answers down. Do not just think them. Writing forces clarity that thinking alone rarely produces. And clarity about where your focus is leaking is the first step toward stopping the leak.

Remember that the comfortable distraction is the most expensive one.

The distraction that costs you the most is rarely the obvious one. It is the one that feels reasonable. The one you can defend. The one that doesn't look like avoidance because it hides in something that appears to be wisdom, preference, or just personality.

Examine your comfortable distractions with the same scrutiny you give your obvious ones. The privacy that keeps you small. The perfectionism that keeps you unpublished. The familiarity that keeps you in the life you have always had instead of the one you are supposed to be building. These are not character traits to be protected. They are patterns to be examined. And if they are standing between you and what you know you are supposed to do with your life, they are distractions. Call them what they are.

Kill the distractions before they kill your goals. The obvious ones and the comfortable ones. The ones on your screen and the ones in your story about yourself.

Especially those.

Chapter 21

THE SECRET TO FINANCIAL FREEDOM ISN'T MORE MONEY. IT'S THIS.

Most people think freedom comes from making more money. And more money helps. But the amount you earn matters far less than what you do with it, and until you understand that distinction at a gut level, your income will never be high enough to feel like enough.

I know this personally. There was a season when I was driving a car I could barely afford the monthly payment on. I looked the part. I had nothing to back it up. The gap between the image I was projecting and the reality I was living was exhausting to maintain, and it kept me from building anything real because every dollar that could have been building something was being spent performing something instead.

You cannot build wealth and perform wealth at the same time. It is one or the other. Every dollar spent trying to look successful is a dollar that is not working toward actually being successful. And the people you are trying to impress are not paying your bills, not losing sleep over your financial stress, and not going to be there when the gap between the image and the reality finally closes in on you.

The moment I stopped performing and started building, everything changed. Not because my income jumped dramatically. Because I stopped hemorrhaging money on things that were costing me the appearance of success instead of the substance of it.

Here is what financial discipline actually looks like in practice.

Know where every dollar goes. Not roughly. Exactly.

Most people have a general sense of where their money goes. General sense is not good enough. General sense is how you end up surprised at the end of the month wondering where it all went while having nothing meaningful to show for it.

Track your spending for thirty days with complete honesty. Every purchase, subscription, and meal out. Every impulse buy. Write it down or use an app, but do not estimate and do not skip the embarrassing ones. The embarrassing ones are the most important because they are the ones you have been ignoring.

What you will find when you do this honestly will surprise you. Subscriptions you forgot you were paying for every month. Food spending that is two or three times what you thought it was because you were counting the restaurants but not the coffee stops and the convenience store runs, and the delivery fees. Small recurring purchases that individually feel insignificant and collectively add up to hundreds of dollars a month, leaving your account without you ever consciously deciding to spend it.

You cannot fix what you cannot see. The tracking is not the punishment. The tracking is the diagnosis. And you cannot treat a problem you have not accurately diagnosed.

Build a budget that reflects your actual priorities, not your aspirational ones.

A budget is not a restriction. It is a plan. It is the document that says here is what matters to me, and here is how my money is going to reflect that before the month begins rather than after it ends.

Most people who try budgeting fail because they build an aspirational budget, one that reflects the person they intend to be, rather than an honest one that reflects the person they actually are right now. They cut food spending to an amount they have never actually hit. They eliminate entertainment entirely because they feel guilty about how much they spend on it. And then real life happens, and the budget falls apart in the second week, and they conclude that budgeting does not work for them.

Budgeting works. Unrealistic budgeting does not. Start with what you actually spend, not what you wish you spent, and build from there. Look at your 30-day tracking honestly and create categories that reflect real life. Then identify the two or three areas where the spending does not match your actual values and make specific adjustments in those areas only. Small, honest changes maintained consistently produce better results than dramatic overhauls abandoned within a month.

Build a buffer before you do anything else.

Financial stress is almost never really about the big things. It is about the absence of margin. When there is no cushion between you and an unexpected expense, everything becomes a crisis. The car repair. The medical bill. The appliance that stopped working. The month in which earnings fall short of expectations. Without a buffer, these are emergencies. With a buffer, they are inconveniences you handle and move on from.

Prior to your investment. Before you pay off debt aggressively. Before you do anything else with discretionary money, build a buffer. Start with one thousand dollars if that feels manageable. Then build toward one month of expenses. Then three months. The number matters less than the habit of maintaining it and not touching it for anything that is not a genuine, unexpected necessity.

The peace of mind that comes from having money set aside for when life happens is worth more than almost anything else you could spend that money on. It changes how you sleep. It changes how you respond to bad news. It changes the dynamic in your marriage when an unexpected expense arrives because the conversation is now how do we handle this rather than how are we going to survive this. That shift alone is worth every sacrifice it takes to build the buffer.

Separate your needs from your wants and be ruthlessly honest about which is which.

This is where most financial discipline falls apart because the line between need and want is one most people draw in a location that is very convenient for their current spending habits. The car you need for transportation is a necessity. The car payment that consumes fifteen percent of your monthly income so you can drive something that impresses people is a want. Housing is a need. Housing that stretches your budget to its limit so you can live in the right neighborhood is a want. Food is a necessity. Daily restaurant meals and premium delivery services are wants.

None of this means you can never spend money on things you want. It means you make that choice consciously with full awareness of what it is costing you, not just in dollars but in options. Every dollar committed to a want is a dollar unavailable for building. That is a trade you may make. But you have to make it with your eyes open rather than pretending the want is a need to avoid the discomfort of admitting what you are actually choosing.

Ask yourself honestly about every significant recurring expense in your life. Is this a need, or is this a want I have convinced myself is a need? The honest answer, applied consistently, will free up more money than most people realize they have been quietly spending on performing a life rather than building one.

Stop spending money to achieve **success.**

This deserves its own conversation because it is one of the most widespread and least discussed financial problems people face. The car that is too expensive. The apartment in the neighborhood you cannot actually afford. People buy everything from clothes and watches to vacations and costly dinners not for their inherent value, but to communicate their identity to others.

The people you are performing for are not tracking your net worth. They do not know what your car payment is. They are not thinking about your financial stress. They mostly focus on their own performance for other people who are equally unaware of them. You are spending real money on a perception that exists briefly in the minds of people who will not remember it tomorrow.

Build reality instead of an image. Drive the car you can actually afford. Live in the home that fits your actual budget. Spend on the things that genuinely improve your life rather than the things that improve your appearance of a life. The person who quietly builds real financial stability while living below their means will always end up in a better position than the person who looks successful while being consumed by the stress of maintaining an image they cannot afford.

Financial freedom is not a number. It is a feeling. And the feeling comes not from how much you earn but from the gap between what you earn and what you spend. Widen that gap intentionally, protect it consistently, and put the difference to work. That is the entire formula.

It is boring. It is unglamorous. And it will change your life in ways that no raise, no windfall, and no investment tip ever could.

Track every dollar. Build the buffer. Stop performing. Start building.

The freedom you are looking for is on the other side of the financial discipline you have been avoiding.

Chapter 22

EVERYONE WANTS FAST RESULTS. THE WINNERS ARE PLAYING A DIFFERENT GAME.

Whatever you are building, a business, a body, a family, a garden, a financial future, it is going to take longer than you expect. Way longer. And the sooner you accept that without resentment, the less of your energy you will waste being frustrated by a timeline you never controlled.

We live in a world that has made patients feel like a character flaw. Somebody blows up on social media and suddenly everyone thinks that is how it works. What they do not see is the three years of grinding behind that one viral moment. The hundreds of posts nobody watched. The failures. The restarts. The days they almost quit. The algorithm did not discover them. Time and consistency finally made them undeniable. There is a difference, and most people miss it entirely.

I think about this every time I walk through my garden. I did not start with great soil. What I have now taken years of composting, amending, learning, failing, adjusting, and showing up to something that gave me very little back in the early seasons. And even now it is still improving. Still not done. The garden taught me patience in a way nothing else could, because a garden does not care about your timeline. You cannot negotiate with a seed. You cannot pressure a root system into developing faster because you are ready for results. You do the work; you create the conditions; you wait, and you trust. That is the entire job.

Your goals work the same way. They will take as long as they take. The question is never how fast can I get there. The question is whether you will still show up when it is finally ready to happen.

Here is how to build the patience and persistence that keeps you in the game long enough to win it.

Redefine what progress looks like.

The reason most people quit before the breakthrough is not a lack of effort. It is a measurement problem. They are measuring progress by outcomes, by visible results, by numbers that move and metrics that change, and when those things do not move fast enough, they conclude that the work is not working.

But in the early stages of building anything real, the most important progress is invisible. The habit being formed. The skill being developed. The soil is being amended. The foundation is being laid. None of these things look like progress from the outside. From the outside, it looks like nothing is happening. From the inside, if you are paying attention, you can feel the compounding beginning.

Change what you measure during the building phase. Instead of measuring outcomes, measure inputs. Did you show up today? Did you do the work? Did you maintain the standard you set for yourself? Those are the only numbers that matter right now because they are the only numbers you control. The outcomes will follow the input. They always do. But only if you stay in long enough for the math to work.

Track your consistency instead of your results. A simple calendar where you mark every day you showed up will show you something motivating after thirty days that no outcome metric can show you yet. The chain of marks is the evidence that the compound effect is building even when you cannot see it anywhere else.

Stop using other people's timelines as your benchmark.

Comparison will make you quit faster than any obstacle you will ever face. You look at someone further along and feel like you are failing. You see their results and forget their process. You see where they are now and assume the distance between you represents a fundamental difference in capability when what it actually represents is a difference in how long they have been at it.

The person with the thriving business has failed more times than they talk about publicly. The person with the strong body has had their own seasons of falling off and starting over. The person with the garden that looks effortless has killed more plants than you have ever owned. You are looking at chapter twenty of their story and comparing it to chapter three of yours. That comparison is not informative. It is destructive.

Social media has made this harder than it ever has been because you now have access to everyone's highlight reel all day, every day. Nobody posts the day nothing grew. Anyone rarely posts content with only twelve views. Nobody posts the financial statement from the year nothing worked. You are consuming a carefully curated version of other people's journeys and measuring your unfiltered reality against it. That is a competition you will never win because it was never real to begin with.

The only comparison that produces useful information is you versus yourself. Where were you six months ago? Are you better? Are you further along? Have you improved your skills, consistency, and discipline over the past year? That is the only scoreboard that tells you anything true. Stay on it and get off everyone else's.

Build your identity around the process, not the outcome.

The people who quit are almost always outcome-focused. They are doing the work to get the result, and when the result does not arrive on schedule, the work loses its justification. The people who last are process-focused. They have built an identity around being someone who shows up, who does the work, who maintains the standard regardless of what the results are doing on any given day.

This is not a minor distinction. It is the entire game.

Tying your identity to the outcome means one terrible month could trigger a motivation crisis. When you tie your identity to the process, you are simply someone who does what you do every day because that is who you are. The results become something that happens to you over time rather than something you are constantly chasing and frequently failing to catch on the schedule you set for yourself.

Start telling yourself a different story about what you are doing. I am not trying to build a successful business. I am someone who builds things and shows up every day, regardless of where things stand. I am not trying to get in shape. I am someone who moves their body and eats well because that is how I live. The shift from trying to being changes everything about how you relate to the days when nothing seems to work.

Prepare yourself for the plateau.

Every meaningful pursuit has a plateau. A stretch of time where the early gains have leveled off, the work has become routine, and nothing seems to change no matter how consistently you show up. The plateau is not a sign that you have stopped improving. It is a sign that you are in the middle of a deeper adaptation that has not surfaced yet.

Beginner gains are fast and visible because the gap between where you started and basic competence is large and closes quickly. The gains that come after that, the ones that build real mastery, real strength, real business traction, real financial stability, are slower and less visible because they are happening at a deeper level. The plateau is where most people quit. It is also where the serious work actually begins.

When you hit the plateau, and you will, do three things. First, acknowledge it without dramatizing it. You are not going backward. You are merging. Second, look for a slight change that might break the pattern without abandoning the foundation. A new variable in the training set . A different approach to the content. A refined financial strategy. Small, intelligent adjustments keep the compound effect moving without starting over. Third, extend your timeline without lowering your standards. Give the process more time. The work is still ongoing. You just cannot see it yet.

Most people quit right before the breakthrough.

This is not motivational language. It is a pattern that repeats itself across every domain and every level of achievement. The breakthrough almost never announces itself in advance. It arrives after a stretch of time that felt like nothing was happening, which is exactly why so many people do not see it. They left just before it came.

The gardener who gives up on a plant two weeks before it flowers. The entrepreneur who shut down the business the month prior to the market's downturn. The content creator who stops posting just two weeks prior to the algorithm finally boosting their work. The person who abandons the financial plan the quarter before the compound interest becomes visible. They were not failures. They were early. And they will never know it.

Stay. Keep working. Trust the process even when the process is giving you nothing back right now. We cannot guarantee a breakthrough on any timeline. But it is far more likely to arrive for the person who is still standing and still working than for the person who decided the wait was too long.

Your thing will take as long as it takes. Show up every day and make sure you are still there when it does.

Chapter 23

YOU'RE COMPARING YOUR CHAPTER 3 TO SOMEONE'S CHAPTER 20 — STOP IT NOW

Comparison is the fastest way to kill your discipline. Not the slowest. The fastest. When you see someone ahead of you, it can trigger feelings of failure. You see their results and forget their process. You see where they are now and assume the distance between you represents a gap in ability when what it actually represents is a gap in time. And then you look at your own situation, the mess, the struggle, the slow progress, and you decide something must be wrong with you.

Nothing is wrong with you. You are just in a different chapter.

After fifteen years, the person whose garden appears effortless has actually killed more plants than you've ever possessed. The person whose body you admire has been consistent for a decade and has had their own seasons of falling completely off and starting over from scratch. The person with the successful business has failed more times than they will ever talk about publicly and has put in years of work you will never see because it happened before anyone was paying attention. You are looking at chapter twenty of their story and measuring it against chapter three of yours. That comparison is not informative. It is destructive. And if you let it run long enough, it will make you quit something you had no business quitting.

Here is what social media is doing to your perception every single day. It is feeding you highlight reels around the clock. Nobody posts their 5 AM struggle. Users do not publicly share content that garnered eleven views. Nobody posts about the garden bed that failed completely. Nobody posts the business idea that went nowhere, the financial mistake that set them back, the season where they fell off everything they had built. You are consuming a carefully curated version of everyone else's journey and comparing it to your unfiltered reality. That comparison was never fair. It was never real. And it is costing you confidence you cannot afford to lose.

You are not behind. You are honest about where you are. That is actually a strength most people do not have. Here is how to use it.

Understand what comparison is actually doing to you.

Comparison feels like motivation because it creates urgency. You see someone ahead of you and you feel the gap, and that feeling looks like it should push you forward. Sometimes it does. But chronic comparison does the opposite. It shifts your focus from your own work to everyone else's results. It makes you feel perpetually behind, regardless of how much progress you are actually making. It trains your brain to measure your worth against an external standard that is constantly moving and completely outside your control.

An athlete who observes everyone else's performance while training on their own will progress less rapidly than an athlete who concentrates entirely on self-improvement. The entrepreneur who is building with one eye on their competitors will decide based on what others are doing rather than what their own customers actually need. The person trying to get healthier while constantly comparing their body to other people's bodies will never feel like enough, no matter how much they improve, because there will always be someone further along to measure against.

Comparison redirects your energy from creation to evaluation. And you cannot build anything significant while you are spending your best mental energy evaluating how your build compares to everyone else's. The focus has to come home. Let's get back to your work. Back to your progress. Back to the only story you actually have any influence over.

Audit your inputs.

You do not accidentally spend hours comparing yourself to other people. You consume content that makes it inevitable, and then wonder why you feel inadequate. The algorithm is not neutral. It shows you content that produces engagement, and comparison produces enormous engagement because it triggers the exact emotional response that keeps people scrolling.

Go through the accounts you follow and ask one question about each of them. Does this make me feel inspired to do my work, or does it make me feel inadequate about where I am? Inspiration sends you back to your own effort with energy. Comparison keeps you on the screen feeling behind. The accounts that consistently produce the second feeling need to go regardless of how much you respect the person or how valuable their content might be in a different season of your life.

This is not about avoiding success stories. It is about being honest about which ones actually serve you right now. The content that makes you want to close the app and go to work is serving you. The content that makes you want to keep scrolling to see more of what you do not have yet is not.

Curate your inputs with the same intentionality you bring to everything else in this book. Your mental environment shapes your output just as much as your physical one does.

Replace the comparison habit with a measurement habit.

The comparison habit exists because you need something to measure yourself against. That need is not wrong. Measurement is how you know if you are improving. The problem is the benchmark, not the instinct. Replace the external benchmark with an internal one and the measurement instinct becomes one of your most powerful tools instead of one of your most destructive habits.

Every week, ask yourself four questions. Was my consistency better this month compared to last month? Have my skills improved over the past six months? Am I further along than I was a year ago? Am I closer to the person I committed to becoming than I was when I started? Those four questions will tell you everything you need to know about whether your effort is working. They will never make you feel behind because they are measuring you against yourself, and you are always ahead of where you used to be if you have been doing the work.

Keep a simple progress journal. Not a detailed daily diary. A brief weekly note about what you did, what improved, and what you are taking into the next week. Over time, this journal becomes evidence. On the days when comparison hits hardest and the feeling that nothing is working is loudest, you can open that journal and see in your own handwriting exactly how far you have come. That evidence is more powerful than any motivational content you will ever consume because it is real and it is yours.

Give people their full story.

One of the most practical ways to break the comparison habit is to stop looking at people's results in isolation and start thinking seriously about what their full story probably includes. Not to diminish their achievements. To accurately contextualize it.

When you see someone with a thriving business, remind yourself that the version of that business you are seeing today is almost certainly not the first version. It is probably not even close to the first version. It is the version that survived multiple failures, pivots, financial close calls, and years of work that produced very little visible return. When you see someone with a strong healthy body, remind yourself that they have a history with that body that includes hard seasons, setbacks, and probably a significant amount of time looking more like where you are now than where they are today.

You are not being naïve when you do this. You are being accurate. Nobody's chapter twenty happened without chapters one through nineteen. Every person you admire has a behind-the-scenes that their highlight reel does not show. Giving them their full story is not generosity toward them. It is clarity for you.

Stay in your lane long enough to see what you are actually building.

The most dangerous thing about comparison is not how it makes you feel in the moment. It is that it can make you abandon something real before you ever find out what it could become. People leave the work, their relationships, the financial plans, the creative pursuits, not because it was not working but because someone else's version of the same thing looked further along, and they mistook position for potential.

Your lane is the only one where your specific combination of experience, perspective, struggle, and purpose is applied to your specific work. Nobody else is building what you are building, the way you are building it with what you have been through. That is not a consolation. That is the actual truth. Your unique experiences allow you to create what you are building in a way no one else can.

Stay in it. Keep working. Stop looking sideways long enough to see what is growing directly in front of you.

Every person you admire started exactly where you are right now. They just did not quit.

Neither should you.

PART FIVE — STAYING DISCIPLINED

Chapter 24

You're Going to Fall Off. Here's Exactly How to Get Back Up Fast.

Let me save you some anxiety right now. You are going to fall off. It is not a question of if. It is when. At some point, you are going to miss a day. Then two days. Then a week. Life will get in the way, or you will get sick, or you will just lose steam. It happens to everyone without exception. And if you do not mentally prepare for it beforehand, it can turn a temporary stumble into a permanent stop.

The distinction between long-term disciplined individuals and those who aren't lies not in the disciplined ones never faltering. It is that they get back on faster. They do not let a bad day turn into an awful week. They ensure a missed workout doesn't lead to a missed month. They stumble, acknowledge it without drama, and start again. That is the entire skill. It sounds simple. It is harder than it sounds because of what happens in your head between falling off and getting back on.

Here is what actually happens and how to handle it.

Understand why falling off feels so catastrophic.

When you miss a day of something you have been consistent with, something happens psychologically that is disproportionate to the actual damage done. The miss feels like evidence. This evidence suggests you lacked true discipline. Evidence that this time did not differ from all the other times you tried and stopped. Evidence that the pattern is who you are rather than a temporary interruption in a practice that is otherwise solid.

That feeling is a liar. One missed day is not evidence of anything except that you are a human being living a real life with real variables that do not always cooperate with your intentions.

The story you tell yourself about the miss matters more than the miss itself. I missed one day is a fact. The story is that I am clearly not disciplined enough. I already ruined it, so there is no point continuing is a story. I might as well start over next month. It is a story. And your brain designs every one of those stories to protect you from the discomfort of getting back up, because getting back up after a fall requires admitting the fall happened and choosing effort, anyway. Your brain would often rather construct a narrative that makes quitting feel logical than face the simple discomfort of restarting.

Catch the story before it takes hold. Name it for what it is. Then do the next right thing.

Apply the one rule that changes everything.

Do not miss two in a row. That is it. That is the rule. One mistake is human. Two misses is the beginning of a new pattern. Three misses is a habit forming in the wrong direction. The gap between one miss and two misses is where the discipline either holds or dissolves, and it is the most important moment in the entire cycle.

You missed your morning routine today. Fine. Tomorrow you are back; no negotiation, no easing back in gently, back to the full standard. You skipped your workout for three days. Go today. Not tomorrow. Today. You ate poorly all weekend. The next meal is good. Not Monday. The next meal.

The rule works because it removes the decision. You are not weighing whether you feel ready to restart. You are not assessing whether the conditions are ideal. You are simply following the rules. You can miss once. Two is not. That binary clarity cuts through all the negotiations your brain wants to have about when and how and whether the time is right.

Write the rule somewhere you will see it. Put it on your phone. Put it on your bathroom mirror. Make it the thing you come back to when the story forms because the story is fast, and the rule needs to be faster.

Know the difference between falling off and needing rest.

Not every interruption in your routine is a fall. Some of them are your body and mind telling you something important that deserves to be heard rather than overridden. The discipline chapter on rest exists for exactly this reason. A person who has been running hard for months and suddenly cannot make themselves do anything is not always being lazy.

Sometimes depletion prevents them from acting, and they actually need recovery instead of a pep talk and a harder push.

Learn to distinguish between the two. Resistance that comes from not feeling like it, from boredom, from the absence of excitement, from the ordinary friction of doing hard things, that is the resistance you push through. Rest that your body is genuinely asking for, the kind that comes with physical fatigue that does not resolve overnight, with emotional exhaustion that has been building for weeks, with a complete absence of energy that differs from your normal experience, that is the signal you respond to with intentional recovery rather than guilt.

Getting this distinction right matters because treating genuine depletion like laziness leads to the burnout that costs you weeks instead of the one or two days of proper rest that could have prevented it. And treating ordinary resistance like depletion gives you permission to stop every time the work gets hard, which is exactly when the work needs to continue.

Check in honestly with yourself when the resistance arrives. Is this I do not feel like it or is this I genuinely need to stop for a moment? Answer that question truthfully and respond accordingly. Both answers are valid. They just require different responses.

Have a restart protocol for each area of your life.

The reason people stay off longer than they need to after falling off is that they do not have a clear picture of what getting back on actually looks like. Getting back on track feels vague and overwhelming, so they keep postponing it until the conditions feel right. The conditions never feel right. The restart needs to be defined in advance so that when the moment comes; you are not deciding what to do. You are just doing what you have already decided.

For your fitness routine, the restart is always the minimum version. Not the full workout you were doing before. The minimum. Twenty minutes. A walk. The garden circuit. Something that counts and gets the streak started again without requiring the full physical and mental resources of a peak session. You will build back to full capacity over the next few days. The restart is just the door back in.

For your nutrition, the restart is the very next meal. Not tomorrow. Not Monday. The next time you eat, eat well. One good meal after a terrible stretch does not undo the terrible stretch, but it starts a new one. And meal built the new one meal the same way the old one was.

For your financial discipline, the restart is opening the app or the spreadsheet and looking at the numbers honestly. Not fixing everything at once. Just looking. Clarity first, then the next right decision from there.

For your relationships, the restart is the next conversation. Not necessarily a big reconciliatory talk . Just showing up present and engaged for the next interaction and letting the consistency rebuild from there.

In every case, the restart is smaller than you think it needs to be. Small enough that there is no legitimate reason to postpone it. Small enough that you can do it today, regardless of how you feel. Start there and let momentum carry you back to full stride.

Stop spending energy on guilt that belongs on getting back up.

Guilt is one of the most expensive emotions you can carry after falling off because it consumes the exact energy you need for the restart. Every hour you spend feeling bad about what you did not do is an hour that is not being spent doing it. Guilt does not build discipline. Action does. The work does not care how bad you feel about missing it. It just needs you to show up.

This does not mean falling off carries no consequence or that you should be indifferent to the miss. It means the response to a miss is a restart, not a period of self-punishment followed eventually by a restart. Skip the self-punishment. Go straight to the restart. You will get back to where you were faster and with more energy than if you spent three days feeling terrible before you finally made yourself begin again.

Be honest about what happened. Name it clearly. Then move. That is the entire process. Anything beyond that is delay dressed up as accountability.

Falling off is part of the process. Every person building something real has a history of falls and restarts that they do not talk about as much as they talk about consistency. The restarts are part of the story too. They are not evidence that you are undisciplined. They are the evidence that you kept coming back.

Staying off is a choice. Getting back up is also a choice. Make the right choice today. The work is waiting for you exactly where you left it.

Chapter 25

Nobody Is Going to Clap for You. Do It Anyway.

The applause you are waiting for is not coming. Not for daily work. Not for the boring, repetitive, showing up even when it is hard work. Not for the 5 AM mornings, the meals you chose carefully, the money you did not spend, the phone you put down, the hard conversation you had, the day you showed up when every part of you wanted to coast.

The world notices the results. It notices when you have lost weight, built the thing, finished the project, raised the kids well. But it does not see the thousands of ordinary days that made those things possible. Those days are invisible to everyone except you. And you let that be enough.

If you need recognition to keep going, you will not last. Because the recognition does not come on schedule. Not for the daily stuff. Not for the consistent, unglamorous, nobody-is-watching stuff. People are busy with their own lives. They are not tracking your progress. They are not cataloguing your consistency. And if your motivation to show up today depends on whether someone noticed yesterday, you are going to run out of fuel constantly.

When I walk in my garden at 6 AM, nobody is watching. Nobody is keeping score when I knock out pushups between weeding. People aren't impressed by my reasonable bedtime instead of staying up late. But I know. I know I showed up. I know I kept my word to myself. And over time, that knowing becomes something more valuable than any external recognition ever could be. You establish a relationship with yourself through this foundation that withstands pressure, as you never built it on others' thoughts.

Here is how to build that foundation practically.

Understand why external validation fails as a long-term **fuel source.**

External validation feels good because it is real. When someone acknowledges your effort, your progress, your consistency, that recognition produces a genuine emotional response. There is nothing wrong with appreciating it when it comes. The problem is building your discipline on the expectation of it because external validation is unreliable as a daily fuel source.

People are busy with their own lives. They are not tracking your progress. They are not noticing your consistency. Your spouse is managing their own load. Your friends are going through their own challenges. If you have followers, they are consuming content in thirty-second intervals before moving on. And if your motivation to show up today depends on whether someone noticed yesterday, you are going to run out of fuel constantly.

The people who last are not the ones who found better sources of external validation. They are the ones who stopped needing it. Not because they became indifferent to encouragement, but because they built something internal, that does not require external input to keep running. That internal engine is what you are building every time you show up when nobody is watching and keep your word to yourself when nobody would know if you broke it.

Build a personal scorecard that only you control.

The most practical replacement for external validation is a personal scorecard that you maintain, review, and take seriously, regardless of what anyone else notices or says. This is not a productivity tracker or a habit app. It is a private record of whether you are becoming the person you said you were going to become.

Define three to five standards that matter to you personally. Not standards designed to impress anyone. Standards that reflect who you are genuinely trying to be. Perhaps it involves showing up to your morning routine without negotiation. Perhaps it involves being fully present with your family during the hours you've set aside for them. Maybe it is maintaining your financial discipline even when spending would be easier.

Maybe it is doing the creative work every day, whether anyone engages with it.

Review those standards weekly. Not to grade yourself harshly, but to stay honest. Where did you hold the line this week? Where did you let it slide? What does this week tell you about the direction you are actually moving? That weekly review, done privately and honestly, becomes your applause. This review is more reliable than anything anyone else can offer because reality, not perception, grounds it. It is also available to you every single week, regardless of whether anyone noticed what you did.

Keep your word to yourself as seriously as you keep it to others.

Most people would never cancel on a friend without a good reason. They would never show up unprepared to a meeting that mattered. They would never break a commitment to someone they respected without feeling genuine discomfort about it. But they break commitments to themselves constantly and feel almost nothing because there is no social consequence. No audience. No disappointment from anyone else. No one is going to bring it up.

That absence of consequence is exactly what makes self-discipline so hard and so important at the same time. You are the only enforcement mechanism. You are the only one who knows whether you did what you said you were going to do. And every time you break the commitment quietly, with no audience and no consequence, you are teaching yourself something. You are teaching yourself that your word to yourself does not carry the same weight as your word to others. Do that enough times and you stop trusting yourself entirely. You stop making commitments to yourself at all because somewhere underneath you already know you will not keep them.

Rebuild that trust the same way you would rebuild trust with anyone else. Keep small commitments consistently before you make large ones. Do what you said you were going to do today, even if it is small, even if nobody will ever know, especially then. Every kept promise is a deposit. Every broken one is a withdrawal. Keep making deposits and watch what happens to your relationship with yourself.

Learn to be your own encouragement.

This is not about positive self-talk in the motivational poster sense. It is about developing the ability to recognize your own progress honestly and give it the weight it deserves rather than waiting for someone else to do that for you.

When you finish a hard week, acknowledge it. Not with fanfare. Just with honesty. That was a hard week, and I showed up anyway. That counts. When you make a difficult financial decision that costs you something in the short term for the sake of the long term, recognize what that took. When you have the hard conversation you had been avoiding, or you get back up after falling off, or you do the work on a day when everything in you wanted to quit, notice it. Name it. Let it register.

You do not need a crowd to validate what is real. You just need to stop dismissing your own effort as though it does not count unless someone else confirms it. It counts. It counted the moment you did it. The confirmation was always yours to give.

Do it for who you are becoming, not for what you have already done.

The deepest reason to keep going when recognition does not come is not about the results you have already produced. It is about the person you are becoming. Every day you show up when nobody is watching, you are casting a vote for a specific person. Disciplined. Reliable. A person whose word carries weight. Someone who does not need an audience to do the right thing. Someone can be trusted because they have proven to themselves in private that they show up, regardless.

That person is being built one invisible day at a time. And five years from now, ten years from now, that person will be so clearly different from the person who needed applause to keep going that you cannot imagine having operated any other way.

The trophy you are waiting for does not exist. The life you are building does. Show up for it every day and let the work be its own reward.

Do it because you said you would. Do it because it is who you are becoming. Do it because the version of your life you are building is worth more than the validation you are waiting for.

Let that be enough. Because it is.

Chapter 26

SMALL THINGS DONE DAILY WILL BEAT BIG GOALS EVERY TIME. HERE'S THE PROOF.

Everything in this book comes down to one truth. Small things done consistently become big things.

That is not a motivational phrase. It is math. And like all math, it does not care whether you believe it. It works whether you are paying attention to it. The question is whether you are going to put it to work deliberately or let it work against you by default.

Most people are waiting for the big moment. The big decision. The dramatic turning point that changes everything at once. And while they wait, the people who understood that there is no big moment are quietly stacking small ones. Day after day. Week after week. Year after year. Until the gap between where they are and where they are becoming is so wide it looks like talent or luck from the outside.

It is neither. It is the compound effect. And it is available to anyone willing to be consistent long enough for it to show up.

Here is what it actually looks like across the areas of life that matter most.

In your health.

Fifteen minutes of movement every day does not feel like much on day one. On day thirty, your body is different. Day ninety, your energy is unique. After a year, your relationship with your physical self has changed in ways that are difficult to explain to someone who hasn't experienced it. The fifteen minutes did not feel significant for any individual day. The accumulation of all of them is undeniable.

The same applies to sleep. Going to bed thirty minutes earlier tonight does not feel like a meaningful decision. Going to bed thirty minutes earlier every night for a year adds up to over 180 hours of additional recovery that your brain and body use to build, repair, regulate, and perform. One small daily decision, compounded over time, becomes a different quality of life.

You do not need a dramatic health overhaul. You need one small improvement made consistently until it becomes automatic, then one more on top of it. Stack enough of those, and the transformation that looked impossible from the starting line becomes the natural result of ordinary daily choices.

In your relationships.

One honest conversation with your child every day builds something by the time they are a teenager that no single heart to heart talk can produce. Trust is not transferred in one moment. It is the result of hundreds of small moments when a parent was present, engaged, honest, and consistent. The child who grows up inside that consistency carries something into adulthood that shapes every relationship they will ever have.

The same is true in marriage. The couple who chooses each other in small ways every single day builds a foundation that can hold the weight of the hard seasons. Not because they avoided difficulty, but because they made enough deposits in the ordinary seasons that the account had something in it when the withdrawals came.

Relationships do not thrive on intensity. They thrive on consistency. The small daily investments that feel almost too ordinary to count are the ones that count the most.

In your finances.

Twenty dollars into savings every paycheck does not feel like building wealth. Over ten years, it is a habit, a buffer, and a foundation that most people never have because they were waiting until they had more money before they started being intentional with the money they already had.

Packing lunch instead of buying it three days a week does not feel like a significant financial decision. Over a year, it is hundreds of dollars redirected from consumption into building. One small, intentional choice repeated consistently rewires how you relate to money in a way that no single large financial decision ever could.

You cannot build financial freedom in one transaction. Accumulating small, disciplined choices, which individually seem insignificant, builds financial freedom. Collectively, these choices create the difference between financial stress and stability.

In your work and your craft.

A year's worth of daily writing, one page at a time, results in a book. One skill practiced for thirty minutes every morning becomes mastery over three years. One piece of content created consistently week after week becomes a body of work that opens doors no single viral moment could have opened. The daily output feels small. The archive it builds does not.

The people who become genuinely excellent at anything are almost never the ones who had the most talent at the beginning. They are the ones who showed up most consistently over the longest period. Talent sets the ceiling. Consistency determines how close you get to it. And for most people, the ceiling is far higher than the consistency they have been willing to bring.

Do the work today. Do it again tomorrow. Let the compound effect handle the rest.

I think back to where I was and where I am now. The difference is not because of one big decision. It is because of hundreds of small ones. Getting up when the alarm went off. Walking in the garden instead of reaching for my phone. Doing the work even when I did not feel like it. Making the hard call in my marriage instead of letting things fester. Being present with my kids instead of being physically there but mentally somewhere else.

None of those things changed my life overnight. All of them changed it.

Before I close, I want to say something about the personal stories in this book.

I did not share them to impress you. I shared them to show you that the person writing this has been in the mess. The financial loss. The identity crisis. The season when everything I had built came apart, and I had to decide who I was going to be in the rubble. I shared them because the first day my mentor ever spoke to me, he did not open with advice.

He opened with a question. He looked at me across that table and asked if I wanted to hear about the hardest decade of his life.

A decade. Not a bad year. Not a rough month. A decade.

And something in me exhaled. Because I treated my own hard season as evidence, the truth that I was simply human left me uniquely broken. We all are.

In the years since that night, I have mentored close to a hundred people. I have sat across from men and women carrying things I would not wish on anyone. And what I have learned from every one of those conversations is something I believe deeply. Life is like a buffet. We all have a plate. And when you actually sit down and look at what someone else is carrying, when you get a real preview of their private weight and private pain, most people quietly make peace with their own plate. Not because their problems are not real. Because perspective has a way of recalibrating everything.

My stories are not special. They are just mine. And I shared them because I wanted you to see that everything you are going through right now has another side. You can reach it. The reset button is always available. The only requirement is that you press it and start. And the vehicle you move forward in is the same one this entire book has been about.

Discipline.

People who know me often ask why a person with my background in health, fitness, and business mentorship also runs a gardening channel. It is a fair question. And my answer is always the same.

It is better to be a warrior in a garden than a gardener in a war.

GrowFitFL was never really about gardening. It is about building the person who can handle whatever life throws at them. Mentally tough. Physically capable. Self-sufficient. Grounded in something real, something they grew with their own hands, something that required patience and consistency and daily attention and gave nothing back to those who quit on it.

The backyard gardener I am building through that channel is someone who understands that you cannot fake a harvest. You cannot negotiate with a seed. You cannot skip the work and still eat. The garden demands exactly what life demands, and it teaches the same lessons this book teaches, just with dirt on your hands instead of ink on a page.

And here is what I know after decades of living at the intersection of these two things. Gardening and discipline are not a coincidence. They are a partnership that goes back to the very beginning of human history. The first man's task was to work in the garden God placed him in. Not as punishment. A purpose. There is something planting, tending, and harvesting that is hard-wired into who we are at the deepest level. This connection re-establishes our link to patience and process. It helps us understand good things require time and consistent care. We cannot force them into existence merely by wanting them badly enough.

That is what I am offering people through that channel. And it is what I have been offering you through every page of this book.

I want to end where this book actually began.

My father worked three jobs and never missed a game. He carried things at work that would have broken most people and never brought a single ounce of it home to his family. He was a man of God, a man of grit, and a man of his word. He did not call it discipline. He just lived it. Every single day. For decades. Without applause. Without a system. Without a book.

He passed away in March 2025. And the silence where that daily phone call used to be is something I carry with me every single day.

But I carry something else, too. Because outside of God, outside of my wife, discipline is the most important thing in my life. More than anything except those two. And I say that knowing I love my kids more than almost anything on earth. Because discipline is how I love them. It is how I show up for them. It is how I became someone worth showing up as.

The old me, the one who convinced himself every night that tomorrow was a better day to start, he does not have this life. This marriage does not belong to him. He does not have this family. He does not have the garden, or the morning routine, or the channel, or the community of people he gets to help every day.

He has excuses. And they are very good ones. And they cost him everything.

The new me is not perfect. I fail, have hard days. I still hear the voice that says tomorrow is better. But I get up. Every day. I do the thing that is hard as if I love it. I keep my word to myself when nobody is watching.

And slowly, quietly, with no one throwing a party about it, the compound effect does the rest.

That's discipline. It is not a personality trait. You are not born either with or without it. It is a practice. Something you build through repetition and the stubborn refusal to stop showing up. A seed you plant in the worst possible soil, in the hardest possible season, and tend every single day until the harvest comes.

And it always comes.

You do not need to be perfect. You need to be consistent.

Start today. Not Monday. Today.

Pick one thing from this book. Just one. Do it tomorrow. And the day after that. And the day after that.

Show up. Do the work. Keep your word to yourself.

The warrior does not wait for perfect conditions. He builds within the conditions he is given. So does the gardener. So do you.

Now do the work.

Acknowledgments

Every book begins long before the first word is written. This one started in a household where discipline wasn't just talked about; it was lived.

The first person I want to thank is God. Not just for the blessings, but for the challenges. For the type of life that gave me the opportunity to develop discipline. And now, by His will, I get to help others see the importance of it. God is good.

To my dad, you showed me what discipline looks like before I ever had a word for it. The way you carried yourself, the standards you held, the example you set - it's woven into everything I do and everything I've written here. This book is as much yours as it is mine.

To my kids, I wrote this thinking of you. I wanted to put into words my path toward becoming a disciplined person, so that one day when you read this, you'll understand that my path wasn't by luck. And neither will yours be. Everything I've built, everything I've pushed through, has been with you in mind. I hope this book shows you what's possible when you commit to the work.

To Toni, my wife, and my partner in everything - thank you for holding things together and for believing in this even when I wasn't sure. You make every version of me better.

To the mentors and voices who poured into me over the years - whether you knew it or not , your lessons lived in me long enough to find their way onto these pages. I'm grateful.

And to everyone who picked up this book looking for more, I see you. Keep going.

ABOUT THE AUTHOR

Jermaine Jefferson is the founder of GrowFitFL, where he teaches people how to grow their own food, take ownership of their health, and build the kind of disciplined life their family can depend on.

Based in West Central Florida, Jermaine grows tropical and sub-tropical food plants and has built businesses using the same principles he applies in the garden. Show up. Do the work. Stay consistent long enough for it to matter.

Beyond the garden, Jermaine leads multiple business and success masterminds where he has helped multiple individuals become millionaires through the same principles in this book principles he did not read about but earned through a lifetime of hard lessons, real failure, and the discipline it took to turn both into something worth passing on.

On his YouTube channel, GrowFitFL, he covers practical food growing, health, and self-reliance. On The GrowFitFL Podcast, he goes deeper into life, discipline, and what it actually means to become the person your family counts on when things get hard. He lives in West Central Florida with his wife and four kids.

OTHER BOOKS BY JERMAINE JEFFERSON

1. **THE FLORIDA PERENNIAL GARDEN** *Easy Plants That Thrive in Heat, Sand, and Humidity*

Florida gardening is not like gardening anywhere else. The heat, the sandy soil, the unpredictable weather most plants do not survive it. This book introduces resilient perennial plants built for Florida conditions that produce food, herbs, and long-term value with far less effort than you expect. Learn which plants thrive, how to grow them successfully, and how to start building a backyard that works for you year after year.

Available on Amazon.

2. **GROW FOOD NOT LAWNS** *Simple Steps to Turn Any Yard Into a Year-Round Garden*

Most yards are maintained for appearance and produce nothing. This book shows you how to change that. Grow Food Not Lawns walks through the practical steps needed to start producing real food at home, even with no experience and limited space. Learn how to design a productive yard, choose the right plants, and build a system that feeds your family season after season.

Available on Amazon.

CONNECT WITH GROWFITFL

For more on growing food, building discipline, and living with intention:

- YouTube: youtube.com/@GrowFitFL

- Patreon: patreon.com/GrowFitFL

- Website: JermaineJefferson.com

ONE LAST THING

You made it to the end. That already puts you ahead of most people who bought this book and never opened it past the first chapter.

Now the real work starts.

If this book challenged you, pushed you, or told you something you needed to hear, take two minutes and leave a review on Amazon. Not for me. Because somewhere out there is a person who needs exactly what you just read and they are still trying to decide if it is worth their time.

Your words might be the reason they stop waiting and start moving.

Thank you for reading.

Now go do the work.

Jermaine Jefferson

Preparation For The King

A

STUDY

OF

SELF-CARE

FAITH

AND

VICTORY

ANN MARIE THRIVES

TABLE OF CONTENTS

Forward
By
Hermien Van Den Berg

Ann Marie and I meet online every week with a small group of like-minded transformation coaches. Our sole aim is to find better ways to serve people with excellence. Technology has afforded us the wonderful opportunity to meet regularly even though Ann Marie lives in the USA and I live in South Africa.

During this time, I have come to know her as a passionate, dedicated, and deeply compassionate person. She is a well of wisdom who readily shares her knowledge and expertise for the benefit of others.

Most impressive about Ann Marie is her deep love for Jesus and people, which has spilled over into the writing of her book on Esther. She has woven years of study, revelation, expertise, and a lifetime of experience into a single work of eclectic writing that aims to encourage, equip, and fortify modern women.

Although millennia separate Esther and Ann Marie's lives, they share a similar struggle. Both of them had to respond with courage to a life-threatening situation. Esther's enemy was Haman, and Ann Marie's enemy was cancer.

Their brave responses leave every woman with a question when faced with a dire situation. How will I respond? Will I go over, or do I go under? You may think you are too weak or timid, but the truth is, within every woman, there is a calling and a longing to rise up. We all want to move forward with faith in the very face of adversity, knowing that we can trust God with our lives.

This book is therefore timely in a much-needed season when we see our world becoming increasingly chaotic. Ann Marie is giving us a blueprint to follow when faced with tests, trials and tribulations and specifically, how to outmaneuver the very enemies that we face. In her case it was not only cancer, but also the tragic loss of family members and friends.

She is more than a life coach, behavioral specialist and author. Ann Marie is a licensed cosmetologist, makeup artist, skin care and essential oil enthusiast. Her specialization in beauty inspired her to also address Esther's lengthy beautification process, in preparation of going into the presence of the king.

As Christians, we share a similar quest. We need to prepare ourselves daily to enter into God's glorious presence. Not only that, we are the bride of Christ. We are destined for the great wedding ceremony where we will one day see the King of Kings face to face. We look forward to that great day and for this very reason, our beautification process matters! It matters inside and out.

Romans 12:1-2 (AMPC)

I appeal to you therefore, brethren, *and* beg of you in view of [all] the mercies of God, to make a decisive dedication of your **bodies** [presenting all your members and faculties] as a living sacrifice, holy (devoted, consecrated) and well pleasing to God, which is your reasonable (rational, intelligent) service *and* spiritual worship.

Do not be conformed to this world (this age), [fashioned after and adapted to its external, superficial customs], but be transformed (changed) by the [entire] **renewal of your mind** [by its new ideals and its new attitude], so that you may prove [for yourselves] what is the good and acceptable and perfect will of God, *even* the thing which is good and acceptable and perfect [in His sight for you].

Introduction

The story of Esther has intrigued me for a long while. As a cosmetologist, makeup artist, skin care, essential oil, and wellness enthusiast, the fact that they had a 12-month beautification process always appealed to me. That, coupled with the amazing journey of a seemingly insignificant woman who became queen while in captivity and saved an entire nation.

During Covid I experienced a lot of changes, as I'm sure the rest of us have. I wanted to take what the Lord was showing me about self-care and mindset and share it with friends. As I started sharing, people wanted more, and I was asked to put it in book form.

This book is the result. Just when I thought it was finished, God led me to add something else. Therefore, what you will see in this book is a bit untraditional.

Having completed several Bible studies on Esther over the past 7 years, you will get the benefit of the revelations I received during those various studies. I hope you enjoy these wonderful insights and unveilings that ignited the desire and calling to write this book, which has been in the making for over a year and used for personal and group studies by friends and clients.

Throughout these years, I also cared for and lost my precious Dad. My brother and three of my best friends also passed away. Woven into this time of tremendous loss, the Lord expanded on the desires deep in my heart. He's knitted them into a wonderful something, made just for me. That fuzzy picture in my mind and prophetic words spoken over me have become the beautiful tapestry of a life I could barely imagine. You could say, like Esther, in unexpected and magnificent ways, God's Name and hand have been all over my life these past years.

In this book, you will get some background and story takeaways, self-care and soul-care tips, my personal journal and prayers while studying.

I've also included a fun "novel" synopsis of Esther from her eyes, how to wait well for what God has for you, and end with a brief story of my finding love.

I pray this book brings you to a place of peace, that it helps transform your life, and gives you strength and courage to do what God has called you to do. To wait on Him, to fast, to find your purpose, and boldly step into the abundant life He has called you to.

Blessings!!!

I.

PRELUDE

Background

The Old Testament story of Esther is a profile in courage and contains many modern parallels for today's over-loaded and stressed woman. The Book gives us lessons of faith, providence and hope so we can be better equipped to live courageously "for such a time as this."

The story of Esther is a historical narrative that takes place in 483-473 B.C., 100 years after the Babylonian exile in Susa, the Capital City of the ancient Persian Empire, now the modern-day Iran. Some Jews have returned to Jerusalem after living in captivity. However, some have stayed. The events in the Book of Esther are confirmed in the Book of Ezra between chapters 6 and 7, and in the Book of Nehemiah and his time period.

This Book is significantly important to Jewish history as it details yet another story of how God saved His favored people, the Jewish nation, from slaughter.

The book of Esther is one of the only two books in the Old Testament that bears the name of the women in them. The other is the Book of Ruth.

Some consider the Book of Esther to be a controversial book as God's name does not appear, nor is mentioned in the entire book. However, His hand is all over it! It repeatedly depicts how God, in His power, sustains and guides human destiny and how He uses people and events to move in supernatural ways. That's His providence! He's always going on ahead to prepare the way for us. In this story, God raises the weakest of the weak, an orphan and a woman, placing her in a position of immense strategic importance.

Every part of this story deals with God's perfect timing. So many little things come together for God's ultimate plan of salvation in the end. The Book of Esther points forward to Jesus as well. There are a lot of similarities to the salvation of God's people and the enemy's plot to thwart that plan of salvation. But God wins in the end and His plan is ultimately fulfilled.

I've often had experiences in my life that seemed to come out of nowhere. There was a lack of understanding and a sense of bewilderment as I wondered where it was all coming from. What I've realized over the years is that God is a God of mercy. He is deliberate, and He uses all things together for our good. There is an enemy. However you want to name it… it could be the devil, satan, oppression, depression, fear, bad karma.

Whatever name you choose for "the enemy," the fact remains that there is one, and we need to recognize that he is NOT for us. But God IS for us and if He's for us, then nothing can come against us. So, all things are turned for good… for all those who love Him and are called according to His purpose. (Romans 8:31 (b) and Romans 8:28)

This story is also about morally compromised people living in an unpleasant world. Although they were in the middle of it, they ultimately chose to follow God.

The Book of Esther starts with worldly greatness. King Ahasuerus' greatness is highlighted in the beginning. The book ends with Mordecai's greatness, shifting to spiritual victory, putting the spotlight on God instead of the world.

Main Characters
(In Order of Appearance)

King Ahasuerus-

I pronounce his name 'are you serious?'

- A very powerful King over a vast empire with a massive territory, ranging from India to Ethiopia (127 provinces) around 483 B.C.
- Was said to be impulsive, not making the best decisions, sometimes in haste and at the advice of his posse

Vashti -

- Queen and wife to King Ahasuerus
- Was banished because she would not oblige the King's outlandish and inappropriate request
- Esther's predecessor

Mordecai -

- Esther's cousin
- Was a wise man and like a parent to Esther when she was orphaned, giving her sound advice throughout the years (we later see that when the advice is needed, it is heeded)
- Was a Benjamite official at the palace gate who loyally served the King

Esther -

- An orphan who lived with her cousin (some translations say uncle)
- Was taught faith and obedience by Mordecai
- A Jewish woman taken into captivity by King Ahasuerus for his harem
- Treated to a year of beauty treatments by Hegai
- Said to be one of the most beautiful women in the harem at that time.
- Showed wisdom and patience throughout her life

- Operated within God's will in a terrible situation, while also dealing with an unpredictable husband
- Humbled herself by putting aside her fears, seeking God and fasting for the salvation of her nation
- Risked her life for her people
- Put her beauty, social grace and wisdom in the service of God's plan, using all of the gifts God gave her
- Was the model of a good daughter
- Carefully weighed Mordecai's advice
- Was a trend/precedent setter calling an entire nation to fast and pray
- Esther then went before the King after having heard from the Lord
- She went forward on a mission like a soldier, even if it meant her perishing
- Birth name was Hadassah (meaning myrtle) but was changed to Esther (meaning star) in order to hide her Jewish/Hebrew origins
- May have been the only one in the harem who did not worship the gods and idols of that culture

- Was in God's hands because she was taught by Mordechai (he did not bow, so she did not bow down)

Hegai -

- The King's eunuch in charge of the harem and other eunuchs
- Showed Esther favor

Haman -

- The enemy - his name, when translated, means "bully." (Have you ever had a bully in your life???)
- Hated Mordecai so immensely that not only did he want to destroy him, but all of his people, the Jews
- Consulted his gods by casting lots, referred to as PUR, to reveal the appropriate time
- Persuaded Ahasuerus to issue a decree that all Jews should be slaughtered on that day and that anyone who killed a Jew could plunder their possessions

Storyline

The Jews were taken into Babylonian captivity by King Nebuchadnezzar. Some of the Jews, like Daniel and Ezekiel, remained in Babylon. Mordecai and Hadassah were taken to Shushan, in Persia, near the Gulf.

The King decided to hold a 180-day feast, with all of the most prominent people of his day, for the purpose of showing his lavishness. Towards the end of that six-month period, deep in his depravity, he was so inebriated that in wanting to win a bet of having the most beautiful wife, he ordered Queen Vashti to come in wearing only her crown.

Vashti refused. The King became furious and the men in his court became afraid. Following the advice of his peers, they had her banished. They chose to make an example of Vashti in the event that any other women would hear of her insolence and choose the same path of disobedience toward their husbands.

Once the King came to his senses, he was full of regret. So they all came up with a plan to find a new queen. Mordecai saw the King's royal edict that beautiful young women would be assembled for the King's harem in Shushan, and that the maiden who pleased the King would take the place of Vashti.

Thought.... Who are you opening the way for? What is God turning for your good?

So it was that Mordecai sent forth his lovely cousin Esther. When she was presented to the King, he loved her above all the women who had been brought before him, and he set the royal crown upon her head.

After Esther became queen, she dedicated herself to the dreams, hopes, and ambitions of her people. She was queen to one of the most powerful emperors in the world. She had sound judgment, exhibited self-control and had the ability to think of others first, thus gaining favor with the people.

Esther, even though she was a queen and lived as an outsider in a hostile environment, was respected by those around her. Just like Joseph and Daniel, they were all taken captive, but had favor with the people around them and in charge of them. They received preferential treatment and were allowed to carry on with their Biblical upbringings.

Esther's life looked great, but was it really? Do things look great for others when you look at them? Do you think they have everything and they are walking on streets of gold on this side of heaven? Yet deep down, one way or another, we all know that the grass is never greener on the other side. If their shades were pulled up, and you could truly see in, the things you imagined that were so perfect about that person's life would soon be put into perspective.

God gave Esther this platform for His divine purpose. God gives each of us a specific assignment, a reason for being here. He uses everything in His scope throughout the Bible... it's all connected and has a specific purpose. Just as He didn't waste a crumb in any of the loaves and fishes miracles, He also does the same in our lives. He doesn't waste any of the lessons, "mistakes" as we call them, or our days of lesser production. He uses them all for our good, and is making great oil in us every day to be poured out in others as we live our lives for Him.

The Israelites, although they were God's chosen people, at various times turned their backs on God and followed other gods. So, who are the closest people around us following? Are we following them instead of following God?

Because of their idolatry, God allowed them to go into captivity. King Nebuchadnezzar, the leader at the time, took them captive. Some, like Daniel, his two famous friends, and many others, were taken to Babylon. Some, including Mordecai and Esther, to Persia.

I think of times throughout my life when I chose to go my own way, apart from God, and it was usually not a good outcome. The Holy Spirit was given to us as a counselor, to guide us into all truth and show us things to come. (John 16:13) But how many of us truly lean on Him for the help we need when we are faced with dire situations?

Once Esther was taken to Hegai for the purpose of being in the King's harem, she went through a year-long beauty ritual for purification that included makeup.

"Each young woman's turn came to go in to King Ahasuerus after she had completed twelve months' preparation, according to the regulations for the women, for thus were the days of their preparation apportioned: six months with oil of myrrh, and six months with perfumes and preparations for beautifying women." (Esther 2:12 NKJV) Some translations interchange the word beautification with the word "makeup."

There were several purposes for those 12 months. One was to thoroughly prepare the women… 3 sets of quarters, four months each, starting with skin care, oils, and final refinement such as clothes, posture, etc. Another purpose may have been to protect the King from any diseases they may have carried into the harem. Also, the King had to make sure that none of them were pregnant, perhaps from someone in their village, before entering the harem, and then claiming that it may be the King's offspring.

They lived their entire lives in anticipation of that one great moment. Most of them, at some point, got to spend one night with the King. Although they were rarely called back, they were expected to be "in waiting" as concubines in the harem. So, in essence, they were taken care of, but really had no life of their own. They were not allowed to marry or have families. They were just in the harem awaiting the possibility of being called by the King.

God's divine timing is all throughout this book. It was only 11-12 months later, as predicted by Haman's casting of PUR, that the plot to kill the Jews was to be put into place by him. This plot, but for Esther, was almost carried out. This is just one example of God's Mighty Hand working "coincidentally" within this Book, without His Name being mentioned once.

II.

ESTHER
CHAPTER FOUR

The "Famous" Chapter

conversation between Mordecai and Esther through the eunuch Hathach....

"As soon as Mordecai heard of the edict that was put in place, he immediately contacted Esther and he asked her to beg King Ahasuerus for mercy. Esther was afraid and replied, "for any man or woman who approaches the king in the inner court without being summoned, the king has but one law: that he be put to death. The only exception to this is for the king to extend the gold scepter to him and spare his life. But thirty days have passed since I have been called to go to the king."

Mordecai replied to her fear... "Do you think that because you are in the king's house you alone of all the Jews will escape? For if you remain silent at this time, relief and deliverance for the Jews will arise from another place, but you and your father's family will perish. And who knows but that you have come to royal position for such a time is this?"

Esther instructed Mordecai "Go, gather all the Jews who are in Susa, and fast for me. Do not eat or drink for three days, night or day. I and my maids will fast as you do. When this is done, I will go to the king, even though it is against the law, and if I perish, I perish." *(Esther 4 - my emphasis)*

On the third day, Esther approached the king. As soon as King Ahasuerus saw her, he held out the golden scepter. "What is it, Queen Esther? He asked. What is your request? Even up to half the kingdom, it will be given to you." This highlights Esther's bravery and the King's love for her. It also shows his impulsiveness to act quickly, before hearing all the facts, considering the consequences, or contemplating the best strategy to handle it.

Thought... Wisdom to understand the time of when to ask and how to ask is very important in how things turn out in our lives.

It had been up to Esther to decide whether she would play the part God offered. Like Moses and

Joseph, in the end, she chose to identify with God's people, even if it meant risking her life to do so. And even though exile was a punishment for Israel's long history of unfaithfulness, God showed that He was still with His people. He delivered and protected them in surprising ways. He repeatedly neutralized their enemies through a series of astounding reversals. Earthly powers were at work to steal, kill and destroy, but a heavenly power, far greater in scope, was at work to save and preserve so they could persevere.

This was a God-ordained event that was years in the making. God went ahead from the beginning of the story to four years in the future. Esther rises to the position of queen with amazing power. Esther manages the power given to her wisely, ultimately bringing salvation to her people.

The story ends with the plot to destroy the Jews being revealed to the King. Haman's hatred toward Mordecai and the Jews was discovered and turned on him. Haman and his family were killed by order of the King. Esther and her people were saved, and they celebrated their victory before the Lord.

As we see from the story, there was a purpose for everything in this Book. Every little detail in it meant something, and God does the same thing in our lives. He wants us to be whole, inside and out. He wants our wholeness to start inside and move to the outside. He wants us to feel and be whole so that our light, which is Him within us, will shine outwardly, permeating everything around us. We are all responsible for our own spiritual and physical well-being.

Now that we've taken care of the spiritual by sharing this beautiful story of God's providence, His love toward us to take care of all things that concern us, let's look at the physical part.

Are we faithful stewards of our bodies and souls?

How do we take care of the vessels He has given us?

III.

BEAUTIFICATION

The Beautification Process

The beautification process required all the candidates for the King's harem to undergo a specific 12 month regimen. This was referred to as "beauty treatment," meaning to scour or polish, and they could not opt out of these treatments.

Because of their closeness to the desert - being subject to sandstorms and the humidity generated from the Tigris and Euphrates Rivers, the women required very specific beauty treatments.

This extremely dry climate was often subject to water shortages, which led to droughts. Therefore, people did not have the privilege of bathing as frequently as we do these days. These beautification processes were a form of cleansing and hygienic exfoliation, followed by a refinement with fragrances.

Hegai's plan was skin care first. Six months of oils would address the troublesome skin conditions that would arise, such as cracking, wrinkling, wind and sun damage, sunburn, and the healing of sores and skin diseases. These environmentally personalized treatments were to help ameliorate the effects of the heat, wind, and evaporation.

Several of the oils available in Esther's time had disinfectant and anti-fungal properties. Because every young woman underwent a thorough oil exfoliation, skin disorders were quickly noted and treated. This would protect the King from being infected by any diseases that could have cost him his well-being and life.

After six months of basic skin care, Hegai and his attendants incorporated oils, spices and fragrances to enhance and refine each girl's natural beauty. The Scriptures do not say whether the popular "cosmetics" of Egypt, such as kohl for the eyes, henna for hair color, pomegranate juice for blush and lip stain figured into the finishing process.

Oils Used in the Beautification Process

omen had daily massages with the following oils because of their specific properties...

Olive Oil...

- Antioxidant and anti-inflammatory
- Soothes inflammation
- Heals burns
- Softens and smooths skin texture

Cassis Oil...

- Derived from cassis berries
- Contains properties for settling PMS
- Subdues emotional flare-ups
- Reduces bloating
- Decreases cramps
- Relieves joint and body pain

Myrrh Oil...

- Listed close to the top of the list of Biblical Essential Oils
- One of the first oils in the Book of Esther
- May have been the most important ingredient in the regimen
- Increases spiritual awareness
- Strengthens memory
- Treats candida, yeast, and ringworm
- Derived from a resin that bleeds from a wound in the bark of a commiphora tree
- Native to Arabia and the Eastern Mediterranean

An extra note for Myrrh Oil... it was given to Jesus as a gift by the three wise men. It is beneficial to women who have just given birth, as it enhances blood clotting and reduces postpartum bleeding. The same oil was also used for embalming Jesus at the time of His death.

I find it interesting that this resin comes from a bleeding wound of the commiphora tree.... Jesus hung on a tree and bled for our salvation... are all of these things coincidences? NOPE!

The resin of the oil has been used for thousands of years as an ingredient in perfume, as incense and as a dressing for wounds. It is also believed to have anti-aging and hormone-like properties. It's reported to stimulate circulation, decrease inflammation, soothe inflamed skin, prevent wrinkles, heal fungal infections, improve oral health, heal mouth sores, alleviate stretch marks, repel parasites and insects.

Ancient Egyptians carried cones on their heads that contained myrrh to prevent sunburn and repel insects (maybe this is where they got the idea for the cone heads 🤣🤣).

Honey was also used as a humectant or moisturizer then and is still used in some natural cosmetics today. It helps retain moisture and is mildly antiseptic. It is also helpful in healing acne caused by hormonal changes.

It contains live enzymes, can sustain human life, and is great for enhanced brain function. Its properties heal, disinfect, and promote uplifting emotions.

Some Tips for Choosing Oils

Use organically and naturally sourced oils with no synthetics. They may cost a little more, but because they are undiluted, they are much better for us.

These pure oils are free of carcinogens and chemicals that disturb our metabolism. A number of oils and aromatics that are listed in Scripture are incorporated into our lives today for greater health and prevention of disease.

They can also help in increasing and maintaining healthy brain function. By acting as an analgesic through the brain's endogenous opiate receptors. These receptors are the body's internal system for regulating pain, reward, and addictive behaviors. They are like the keys that unlock our brains. The oils simulate the effects of aspirin or morphine. They aid in calming our minds and bodies, helping to keep our spirits light in order to move easily through life.

Some oils can be applied directly to the skin or ingested in water, tea or favorite beverage. Others need a carrier oil as they are considered to be hot oils which can burn the skin when applied directly.

A carrier oil can diffuse the heat in the essential oil so it can be "carried" to the skin and body safely. Some effective carrier oils are coconut, sweet almond, jojoba, and grapeseed. These oils are best when cold-pressed or cold-expeller pressed. With the exception of jojoba oil, these oils maintain their integrity and effectiveness when kept in a cool, dark place.

Citrus oils such as orange, lemon, lime, and grapefruit contain compounds known as furanocoumarins that when exposed to sunlight can cause skin sensitivity. Therefore, it's best to use these oils when you know you will not be exposed to sunlight.

Most essential oils come with instructions either on the bottle or box. Please check for best use, whether topical, ingested or diffused.

Why We Need a Beautification Process

It's been discovered that 80% of our aging process comes from our environment and only 20% is from our DNA. That means that our environment has more of an impact on our aging and hydration than our genes do. So, like the people in Esther's day, we are also subject to our environments.

However, we have more control than we may think. We can use products that are beneficial to our skin in keeping it clean, exfoliated, hydrated, and protected. This will help reduce fine lines, making them less noticeable for those selfies we love to take and share with others. You too can have great skin without the filters on your phone.

Our beauty is both inward and outward. Our inward beauty comes from our relationship with God and how we choose to handle what happens in our lives.

The experiences that we are confronted with in life mold and shape us. Our outward beauty comes from the habits we practice and the self-care products and methods we choose to invest in to treat our bodies well.

As a coach, I teach people how to break habits that do not serve us and implement good habits that do. The reversal and replacement of a habit takes about 63 days. One 21 day period to break the habit and replace it with another, and two 21 day periods to make the habit "stick." This also gives time for the new habits and treatments to be felt and seen.

Our Physical Beautification Process Matters

There are five self-care components that our skin needs in order to keep those lines to a minimum and sustain a healthy glow.

The first is to *cleanse*. Proper cleansing removes dirt, oil, and impurities that we collect while we sleep, and while we're out and about in our daily activities. Free radicals (agents that can damage and age skin) are everywhere, even in our homes. Therefore, it's important to rid ourselves of those elements regularly and have fresh, clean, and line-free faces.

The second is to *exfoliate*. Our skin is always regenerating and when old skin is not sloughed off, the new skin cannot shine forward. Dead skin also piles up, dulling our skin's appearance and causing fine lines. So, choosing a good exfoliant and using it 3-4 times a week will help to maintain your skin's radiance and suppleness, and keep those lines at bay.

The third is to *tone or freshen*. This completes the cleansing and exfoliating processes, and closes the pores. The pores are still breathing, but no longer susceptible to dirt getting in easily. Many cleansers have incorporated ingredients to accommodate for toning. So, if you're not inclined to do an extra step, choose one that has this extra component.

The fourth is to *hydrate*. This step helps to keep the skin from drying or getting too oily, and it helps in minimizing the aging process. Using a hydrator with a sunscreen, for those who can, is a bonus.

Finally, our fifth step is to *protect*. This usually involves a foundation, and it is a crucial step as it ties the others together and finishes things off. When people hear the word "foundation," they sometimes get apprehensive.

Gone are the days of cake makeup and having discolored jawlines that denote that you are wearing something and not sporting your bare skin. I prefer to use a foundation that gives me just a little color to even out my skin tone. There are many formulas to choose from... liquid, powder, CC Cream, with or without sunscreen, etc.

The best products to use for maximum results are any products that have more than one benefit and fall into the category of the five components the skin needs. Let's keep it simple and work smart for our skin. It only takes about 10 minutes a day to take care of your skin, including morning and evening, without makeup. So stop thinking about it and just do it.

To increase the effects of rejuvenation, choose products and ingredients that will help you maximize the impact of your regiment's investment. Ingredients such as retinols, boosters, and special vitamins, such as A, C, and E (ACE, a great acronym that is easy to remember) will help enrich your skin's look and feel and prevent premature aging.

Remember....

The aging process is 80% environmental vs. 20% DNA. So ultimately, you are in control.

That means YOU make the difference, not your ancestors. Take stock of the environment you live in and create for yourself.....

- Your climate matters
- Where you work matters
- What's around you matters
- What you eat matters, the types of foods you choose.... processed vs. fresh/organic, properly sourced
- What you drink and how you choose to hydrate yourself matters... coffee vs. tea, water vs. soda, juices or energy drinks

YOUR WHOLENESS MATTERS....

What you think and how you nourish yourself physically, spiritually and emotionally have an impact on your overall wholeness.

Our Spiritual Preparation for Him Matters

Just as there are five essential self-care components for the care of our skin, these same steps can be applied to the successful cultivation and preservation of our relationship with God and our healthy spiritual glow. Self-care and soul-care go hand in hand as it's important to care for our bodies both inside and out. Let's take a look at our spiritual beautification steps.

Cleanse.... coming clean with God is important to our relationship with Him and the health of our souls. When we ashamedly hide things, come in fear because of sin, are dishonest, and do not put our full heart before Him, it clouds our spiritual walk and fellowship with Him. Cleanse yourself to get rid of the impurities that can create barriers between you and God by consistently introspecting, being mindful of unhealthy behaviors, negative thoughts, emotions, and actions that are contrary to the Word of God. Be sure to check on your forgiveness meter, do you need to forgive yourself or others? Be quick and consistent with these steps so that things don't get clogged, create back up, and produce guilt and shame which can cause us to hide from God like Adam and Eve did in the garden. (Genesis 3:8) He loves you and no matter what state you are in, you can always go boldly to Him.

Exfoliate... this step involves getting rid of things that are dead to promote healthy regeneration. In 1 Corinthians 13, the Apostle Paul talks about putting aside childish things and things that don't serve us, so we are free to serve and fellowship with excellence. In order to have a strong spiritual walk and deepen our faith, we would do well to take an inventory of our days and hearts and eliminate what is no longer purposeful. Think of it as a 10-pound sack of sugar on your back... do you really want to carry all that dead weight around? Let go of guilt, shame, and unforgiveness. When we hang on to what's dead, there's no telling when or where the stench will manifest itself.

Toning and Freshening... in the natural, when we cleanse and exfoliate, our new skin is exposed. Therefore, we must close the pores so that impurities don't get in, causing them to get dirty again. It's the same way in the spiritual realm. Once you've done the first two steps, guard yourself by closing the door to those things that easily trip you up. Refresh yourself in Him and close out the things of the world. Stay in a state of fellowship throughout the day so that you don't fall prey to the little foxes that are around you that want to get under your skin and steal your peace.

Hydrating.... Jesus refers to Himself many times in Scripture as the Living Water. He told the woman at the well that the water He could give her would keep her from ever getting thirsty again. He is *the* Living Water, which means it's ever-flowing because it's alive, with capabilities for continual refreshment. Draw near to Him to be hydrated by the water of the Word and your fellowship with Him. Just as hydration of our skin and bodies sustain our life, so does going to the well to draw out His water. Our bodies can go longer without food than they can without water. Go to the well in prayer, supplication, drinking in His peace, and the refreshment that only His living water can provide. (John 4:10-14)

Protect.... as we take steps to protect our faces and bodies, let's not forget to protect our souls. What does protecting your soul look like? Continuing in the steps above by avoiding the things of the world that would hinder your relationship with God. It's always good to check ourselves, being mindful of the behaviors and choices that cause us to wander from Him and keep us from having honest, meaningful fellowship. Let's protect ourselves from the things that cause us to fall, become ashamed or guilty, ultimately hindering our relationship with God. For me, one of the things I watch is my inner circle. Who are the people and things I let into my life? When I encounter situations that I cannot make sense of, I seek the help of the Holy Spirit first, then wise and godly counsel. He especially keeps me in check because I know in my heart when I'm going against Him. Practicing these steps protects my walk and keeps my walls secure. Like a city without walls is a man without self-control. (Proverbs 25:28)

Managing ourselves throughout the day and keeping ourselves in check is the key to avoiding the escalation of circumstances because you're nipping things in the bud before they progress.

Preparing for Him also involves trust and confidence. We must trust that He truly loves us and wants our best. We must know that He is for us and not against us. (Romans 8:31) We must understand that everything we've ever needed for our earthly walk is already inside us, and only when we join our lives with Him will we THRIVE in this one, until we see Him again. All the beauty, all the peace, all the joy is in us and flows through us when we allow His peace and strength to permeate our souls and lives.

IV.

SELF-CARE
ISN'T SELFISH

My Self-Care Story

*L*et me start with saying… "self-care isn't selfish."

The earliest use of makeup can be traced back almost 7,000 years. Archeologists found canisters of makeup in Egyptian tombs. It's said that Cleopatra created lip color from ground carmine beetles to create a hue (yuck… necessity truly is the mother of invention 🤣🤣).

We have two spectrums of self-care these past few years since Covid. One, where people who never really practiced, self-care are now starting to take better care of themselves, as the media has acknowledged its potential to spur wholeness and mental health. And some have gone in the other direction, where they've relaxed on their self-care because their brains are in a fog and they no longer have the structure in their lives to continue to implement the things that were in place before.

I frequently stay in check by reminding myself of my intentions for self-care. With the help of the Holy Spirit, I try to stay within the scope of being a good steward of the body the Lord has given me.

I frequently ask myself the following questions:

What are my intentions for self-care? Are they so I can mask what's going on inside me? Is it to take care of myself and the temple God gave me? Is it to look better in front of others?

For me, proper skin care and body care is my way of worshiping God, stewarding the temple He has given me that He now chooses to live in. Is my practice always perfect? By no means, I am human.

Sometimes I want to mask what's going on inside of me, kind of like keeping my face fresh while fasting so that I'm not displaying everything that's inside to the outside. Other times, I want to look better for those around me.

One thing that was a challenge for me when I was going through cancer was all the doctor's appointments. I was feeling spent inside. Then I would walk into the medical offices and see people in scrubs, like they'd just rolled out of bed and come to work. There wasn't a sign of self-care sight. Pale faces, thrown up hair, attitudes that were less than pleasing, and sometimes it made the process of what I was going through a little more somber.

However, it lightened my day and mood to see people who were not only cheerful on the outside, but cheerful on the inside. It showed that they not only cared for themselves, but cared for those who they would come in contact with throughout the day.

The intention of why we do anything comes from our hearts and is what matters most to God. The fact that God lives within me is something I try to remember every day. Honoring Him and finding hope from within, is my staple, especially when it seems that the very purpose of everything around me is trying to draw me away from Him and His truth. My resolve in taking care of myself is to offer that to Him and to others.

I'm not sure when this passion started, but it eventually led to me becoming a licensed cosmetologist and makeup artist. Becoming a beauty consultant and helping women take care of their skin, finding products that were suitable for their skin type and coloring was very fulfilling to me.

My earliest self-care memory was asking my mom to buy me Camay soap so I could keep my skin clean. Instead, it created a rash. Then I switched to Ponds Cold Cream, which worked for a while, until it didn't. And who's heard of Noxema?

The point is, there was a deep and innate desire to care for myself. I was intuitively in search of something to wash my face with because that was one of the first things that people saw and I wanted to care for it so it would look good on the outside.

I was struggling on the inside and everything about me screamed, "look away." I wanted so much to fit in and be accepted. I got past that stage and eventually just wanted to look good for myself.

Using special products was and still is one of the solaces of my life. Taking care of my skin... the washes and lotions for my body, along with fun products for my face and hair, made life a little more bearable to me.

I was excited when I eventually found the things that worked for me at the age of 16. Being a bit of an artist, I enjoyed painting my eyes and lips. It was fun and therapeutic for me to match my colors to my wardrobe. It made me feel good on the outside, which made the inside feel better.

I know it's the reverse of the norm, as it's best to work on ourselves from the inside out, and I was doing the opposite; but at the time it was what was best for me, and I was grateful for this little comfort that brought me peace in a time of turmoil.

Coming from years of bullying for different reasons when I was younger, taking care of myself gave me some sort of self-worth and confidence. Practicing good skin care, using a special body wash or shampoo, for me were antidotes that aided in forgetting the words that other people shouted at me, even if it was for just a little while.

The deeper I got into the Word and in my spiritual walk, the more I realized that our beauty radiates from the inside. No matter what color hair or eyes you have, how much you weigh or how tall you are, YOU ARE BEAUTIFUL!

No amount of makeup or the most talented of makeup artists can conceal a dark soul. The truth always comes out. When you are beautiful on the inside, you radiate beauty on the outside. The preparation and purification of our souls is beautiful in God's eyes and in the eyes of others because there is no way to mask or dim a light that is shining from the inside out.

Yes, Esther had a beautification process, but that process started long before she was taken into the harem. Mordecai had taught her the principles of God, and her faith was strong. That faith caused her to have favor everywhere she went because the beauty was in her soul and that radiated to every part of her life. Let that same spirit be within you. Start from the inside out.

Some Things to Ponder

Have you found yourself in a unique place of influence in your life? What have you done with that opportunity?

What are your first actions when unsettling news comes your way? What are some of your first words?

Do you believe that God is omnipotent? That He is our ultimate provider?

That His almighty provision is 360, full circle, encompassing our past, present and future?

Going on ahead of us, knowing what is there, and making the exact provision for us so that we are completely taken care of when we get there?

The King needed to put his scepter out in order for anyone to be accepted before him.....

Jesus is the Scepter that God puts out for us to enter into His divine presence. Without Jesus, and the grace we received by accepting Him as our Savior, we could not enter into God's presence in the Holy of Holies. Because of His sacrifice, we can go boldly before His throne, repeatedly, with no one to hold us back but ourselves.

The Importance of
our First Responses

*F*or Esther, and maybe at times for us too, the first response may be a bit of fear, or we speak and rehearse the current state of the situation. "If I go before him without being summoned, I could die." After being coached, or given a word from the wise who have gone before us, we may see another perspective. Who knows if God didn't put me here just for this? Whatever "this" is, we have to examine and face it from where we are and see what God has for us in "it".

- Everything that is put in our path is there for a purpose.
- A helpful question for ourselves is, why is it approaching me now?
- Is it meant to bless or curse me?
- Then we can reach into our toolboxes and ask "is there a Scripture regarding this?"

- Did something in my past prepare me for this?
- If so, what lesson can I apply to this situation and how can it change my life and the lives of others?
- What do I throw away?
- What do I keep?

I have found that it's best to use these approaches when something seemingly out of the ordinary comes at me.

The Big ASK

*D*o you put all of your cards on the table when something happens in your life? Do you give your pearls to swine without assessing the situation and then regret all the yuck that you just spewed? Esther was wise. She listened to the Holy Spirit. She went to the King strategically.

She appealed to him in his own language, recognizing his desires and methods of communication. She gained more of his trust by speaking of things that were important to him. She took the time to read the room, to see what was happening, not just coming with her own agenda, as life threatening as it was, and she spoke appropriately for that specific moment.

This is not a form of manipulation. It's understanding a situation and using wisdom to act in the best interests and outcome of all those involved. Her wise approach and prudent actions warmed the heart of the King, reminded him of his love for her, and produced the most beneficial outcome for an entire nation and generations to come.

Think about it, Esther could have had anything she wanted, but what she wanted most was the safety and salvation of her people. This was worth far more than any "thing" the King could monetarily and materially have to offer.

Can you think of a time in your life where everything worked out for your good?

Can you look back and see how everything was prearranged for you?

That what you learned and did before this happened has prepared you for this time? That you were already guided into all truth, through the Holy Spirit, and you used that truth to help you in this situation?

Do you see how, even though you were swimming in unchartered waters during this time, something seemed familiar and guided you through?

Do you celebrate and make markers in your life when God delivers you from something?

God asked the Israelites to wear special things, use stones, and other methods as remembrances of His glorious workings and miracles in their lives.

Do you take the time to thank Him, to worship Him, and celebrate Him for how He's pulled you through?

Like the leper who came back, take time to thank Him for all the takeaways that you now have. They are tools for your toolbox, to bring you peace and to help you overcome what may be upcoming in your life. These tools can be beneficial to you and to those around you.

Let the Holy Spirt inspire you to trust God's wisdom and timing. To stand strong in the face of whatever may be coming against you. Let Him remind you that everything has a "name" and that "name" has to bow down to the Name of Jesus.

Only with Him and in Him can you overcome anything that is coming against you.

V.

CHAPTER REVIEWS AND TAKEAWAYS

Reviews and Takeaways

Chapter 1

The Book begins with the story of King Ahasuerus and the events that took place when he held a 180 day celebration. That's 6 months of partying where the King displayed his lavishness and had servers and staff that attended to the guests' every whim.

The author goes on to characterize the lavishness of his palace, painting pictures of the marble pillars, purple curtains, etc. (anything made with a purple dye was expensive at that time). Drinks were served in golden vessels. There was royal wine, extravagance, and extreme wealth. Whatever the people wanted, they got. Among those in attendance were seven of the highest-ranking men in Persia, who were also part of the King's inner circle.

After a week of indulgence, while the King was in a drunken stupor, he asked Queen Vashti to do something inappropriate. She refused. He was furious and had her banished. At the advice of his cohorts and experts in legal matters, a decree was made, and an order given for all women to honor their husbands and obey their orders or face similar consequences as Vashti. This decree was sent out to all the provinces.

In those days, once laws (decrees) were written, they could not be repealed. They were set in stone, unless another law was made abolishing the first.

Chapter 2

King Ahasuerus begins to sober up and comes to his senses. He realizes what has happened and is having second thoughts. Again, his peers step in to help him in making decisions and they suggest and implement a six-point plan…

- Maidens were sought for the King to take the place of Vashti
- Officers in the 127 provinces of his kingdom were put in place to execute the plan
- The officers were to gather all the "fair young virgins" and bring them to the Shushan palace
- The women were to be placed in the house for women in the custody of Hegai, the King's chamberlain, the keeper of the women
- They would go through a customary, twelve-month purification process
- The woman/maiden who pleased the King would become queen in place of Vashti

This quest to find a replacement for Queen Vashti may have started the first "beauty contest" while in essence, building a harem for the King. Mordecai and Hadassah (Esther) are introduced. They are from the line of Benjamin.

Esther is brought to the palace harem and Hegai, the eunuch in charge, took a special interest in her. He gave her beauty treatments, ordered special foods for her, assigned her seven personal maids from the palace, and gave them the best rooms.

At Mordecai's request, Esther did not reveal her lineage or background. Mordecai checks on her daily.

It's now Esther's turn to go into the King and she asks for help and gleans from the wisdom of those who taught her in order to be her best.

The King ends up falling in love with Esther and placing a crown on her head, making her the new Queen and there was a great wedding celebration.

Chapter 3

The King promotes Haman, an Agagite, making him the highest ranking official in government.

It's important to note here that the Agagites were descendants of King Agag, who was the last remaining survivor of the Amalekites. King Saul was given an order to kill all of them. Saul practiced *partial* obedience. He kept Agag alive and even though Samuel eventually killed him, the Agagite race carried on and Haman was one of their descendants. Had Saul obeyed, there may not have been a Haman and a plot to kill the Jews.

What has God asked you to do that you partially or completely disobeyed, and now, you and possible generations after you are reaping from that seed?

Haman is extremely proud, desiring glory for himself. He wanted everyone to like him and bow down to him. Mordecai would not bow down, and so he developed a disdain for Mordecai... to the point of wanting to not just kill him, but all of his people too. Funny thing about hatred. If you let it persist, it will permeate your entire life and the life of those around you.

Throughout the Bible and secular history, there is a woven thread of satanic, Anti-Semitic, strategic plots to kill the Jews because the enemy knew that they were God's chosen people and that the Messiah was coming from that lineage.

The enemy wanted to ultimately destroy and thwart the promise of God to bring a deliverer to His people. Even after the crucifixion of Jesus, with regimes such as Hitler's, other enemies in their own nation, and nations around the world, God's chosen people are still being persecuted and executed.

Haman is now casting lots (PUR… the Persian word for lots used to conjure when the most favorable time would be to do something). He is plotting the destruction of the Jews, which, according to the lots cast, is to take place during the Jewish feast of Passover. Five years have passed since Esther was crowned queen, and nine years since the beginning of this story.

Haman goes to the King with a very vague and deceptive plan, also promising to give the King money, never mentioning in detail that it was for the massacre of the Jews. King Ahasuerus blindly agrees to it without seeking further information.

We are seeing more of King Ahasuerus' patterns of being swayed by people around him, especially when he's angered or drunk. He gives Haman his signet ring (used to seal official documents) and says "do what seems good to you," pretty much giving Haman power of attorney.

Haman immediately goes through all the 127 provinces to get the edict out there to expedite his agenda. According to the lots cast, they only have 11 months to put this plan into place. While King Ahasuerus and Haman are eating and getting drunk, the people in the provinces are distressed, confused, and in turmoil because the Jews were good neighbors who caused no trouble.

Chapter 4

Mordecai learns what has happened at the palace, rips his clothes, and puts on sackcloth and ashes. These were Biblical expressions of grieving in their culture, and all the Jews knew what Mordecai was doing and followed suit, joining him in his mourning.

Esther sends Hathach the eunuch with clothes for Mordecai so he could cover up and to find out why he was wearing sackcloth. Mordecai sent back word about what was happening, along with a copy of the edict that had just been put into place.

The communication goes back and forth as Esther sends word back to Mordecai through Hathach. She explains the rules of going into the King without being summoned. And since he's already a crazy man, she hesitates and explains to Mordecai why she cannot go in (as if he doesn't already know).

The law was absolute. There was strict court etiquette, making Esther's task to go in to the King even more difficult, as it had been five years since her coronation and a month since the King had summoned her.

Now we come to some of the most famous lines in the Book of Esther. The fate of the Jews was in God's hands, not in Esther's, but she was needed to carry it out. If you don't speak up, relief and deliverance will rise from someone else. But you and your father's house will perish. A gentle reminder that God is faithful no matter what, but there are consequences for our disobedience.

God wants to work through us. Esther's own well-being was dependent upon her obedience. God's purposes will not be thwarted. They will prevail, independent of our own obedience. However, He continually gives us opportunities to participate in His redemptive process.

God strategically places us according to the purposes of His providential timing. Esther's fear was valid, but the very reason she was there at that moment was for the specific purpose of saving the Jews.

Do not be afraid of those purposes and opportunities that God puts before you. It's for those very purposes that God has called you. That's why those things are there and they are specific to you.

Every day we are faced with invitations from God to participate in His plans. Throughout our lives, the purposes unfold, showing us more of His plan for us, those around us, and which piece of the puzzle we are in each scenario.

Is it a coincidence that approximately two million women were taken, and that Esther was part of the 400 that were groomed for the King's harem? Or that Mordecai is stationed at the gate, at this specific point in history? The people Esther was surrounded by, their stations in life, their geographical locations, were all meaningful and purposeful.

God wants to use every detail of our lives for His purposes. Nothing is by chance, even when it looks like it might be.

Esther asks Mordecai to gather all the Jews, hold a fast, and then she would go to the King, even if it costs her life.

Chapter 5

Three days pass and Esther gets ready to see the King. She puts on her royal robes and wisely stands in the outer court where the King may notice her, in hopes of calling her in. He sees a glimpse of her and puts out his scepter, granting her permission to enter the inner court. Her favor with the King was evident. Not only did he invite her in, he asked what she wanted, and said he would give her up to half his kingdom.

Despite the imminent plight of her people, Esther maintains her composure and asks the King to just have a meal with her and invite Haman. The King agrees and they have their first feast.

Haman leaves a happy man, only to be infuriated by Mordecai ignoring him and not bowing down to him as he passes through the palace gate. Despite all his accomplishments, this one thing is eating at him. It causes such hatred within him that he complains to his family and they all plot to kill Mordecai.

Chapter 6

This chapter begins with yet another "coincidence." The King cannot sleep and orders the journals of events to be brought to him. He reads about the plot to kill him that was intercepted by Mordecai. He asks those around him what was done to honor Mordecai for saving the King's life and he learns that no reward was given.

Haman happens to be in the court while this is happening. The King asks him what should be done for a man who the King wants to honor. Haman, being the shy man that he is, thinks of himself and comes up with this exorbitant plan of things that he'd like done for him if he were to be honored.

The King agrees with Haman's plan and says, "Great! Go do that for Mordecai!" Hot coals anyone??

The remainder of the chapter is about Mordecai's exhortation and Haman's mortification. Haman returns to his home and starts recounting to his family and friends what happened. They suggest that he doesn't stand a chance against Mordecai and that he should build gallows and hang him.

Chapter 7

This chapter opens with Esther's second dinner with the King and Haman. While they are eating and drinking, Esther carefully approaches the King, strategically revealing the plot to kill the Jews and also reveals that these are her people, and she is in danger as well.

King Ahasuerus asks who came up with this plan and Haman is exposed. The King becomes furious, leaves the room momentarily and when he comes back, he sees Haman before Esther, begging for his life. Some translations say that Haman was grabbing for Esther's clothing. This further angered the King as he thought that Haman was assaulting Esther.

Harbona, one of the eunuchs, spoke up and pointed the King towards the gallows that Haman had built to kill Mordecai and the King, in turn, gave the command to hang Haman on them.

And so it was done!

Chapter 8

Queen Esther was given Haman's estate and Mordecai was given the highest-ranking position in the palace, short of the King.

Esther collaborates with the King to put a new law in place to override the edict to kill the Jews. He granted her request, and the law was posted throughout the 127 provinces.

The new law also authorized the Jews to arm and defend themselves on the day that was cast by PUR for them to be annihilated. This causes the fear of the Jews to rise among the people around them. Some even become Jews because of the favor that was upon them and so they would not be killed themselves.

Mordecai puts on his royal robes and walks out of the palace for all to see; there is a grand celebration among the Jews.

Chapter 9

On the very day of their proposed destruction, the tables were turned and the Jews in the 127 provinces overpowered those who longed for their demise. No one could stand against them. The government officials who served the King even helped defend them. Haman's ten sons were also killed and their dead bodies were publicly displayed.

The Jews fought for 14 days, but did not take any plunder. They celebrated on the 15th day and gave each other gifts. They called for an annual celebration on the 14th and 15th days of Adar, to celebrate their relief from their enemies. As depicted in other Scriptures, their mourning was turned into dancing.

Mordecai became a powerful leader and gained more respect from the people around him.

Chapter 10

This chapter begins with the King imposing taxes and tells of the King's accomplishments, which can be found in The Chronicles of the Kings of Medes and Persia.

Mordecai ranked second in command to the King and was very popular and respected.

Unlike Haman, Mordecai was a wise and powerful leader, revered by the people.

Novel Fun - Day 1

What has God called you to that you need to stand up for? Are you standing up for your time? The calling on our lives must be prayed for and stepped into. It's not always easy to believe and move forward with the plan God has for you, but you are not alone.

The God who created you knows what's inside you and what He's called you to. Lean into Him, His spirit and His goodness to you so that you can gain the strength, wisdom and blueprint to follow His plan.

Let Him draw it out of you and put it into action. Continue to lean in along the way and He will direct your every step. Be the Esther that is in you so that you can save the people that God has assigned you to help. Step up to YOUR CALLING!

Novel Fun - Day 2

Have you ever been called to do something or ask something of someone that terrifies you?? How do you prepare for "The Big Ask?" Do you do your makeup and make sure your hair is perfect? Do you put on that dress that makes you feel special with all of the accessories so that when you walk in, you are noticed, taken seriously and given favor?

Even when we approach *The King,* God, we go in under the veil of Jesus… we get to go in boldly because of His sacrifice and we are received because of our faith in Him. We must go in prepared, just like Esther… but our dress is the cleansing of Jesus and our faith will be what pleases God. Faith in Jesus to enter and faith in God's Word to go boldly before that throne and make that BIG ASK.

He hears us, He always hears us… just as Jesus, who started His prayer for Lazarus in the same way, we must be confident that our Father will hear us and make all things work together for our good.

Have faith in God like Esther, prepare yourself spiritually and physically and take on what God has for you for such a time as this.

Novel Fun - Day 3

When faced with a situation that you don't know how to handle, what do you do? Do you become hopeless, retreat, cry, freeze? What happens to your mind and body? Do you make excuses for yourself and run around in circles in your mind or maybe state the facts as they are, forgetting to factor God in?

Esther, when asked for help with an evil plan of the possible annihilation of her people, started quoting the facts, not what she saw. That was her first response... I haven't seen the King in over 30 days and anyone who goes in without being summoned gets executed.

Mordecai asked her a question which snapped her to reality. A word was spoken that caused her to stop and see the situation in a different light. She realized it was bigger than her, and that she was in an exceptional position, like no one else was.

When you don't know the answer, seek God. Ask Him what He would have you do. Look away from the situation for a moment and look at Him.

Raise your eyes, arms, and heart to Him. The answer always comes. Count on His love and His mercy. He loves you and wants to protect you and show you the way.

Novel Fun - Day 4

Who do you run to when it all falls down?

Esther was wise enough to understand that she was in a very precarious position, and so were her people. She saw that everything that she had gone through to get to this position, like Joseph, had put her in an advantageous position and that now, all her suffering, her heartache, her captivity, was beginning to make sense.

There was a light at the end of this tunnel. She probably looked back at her life, the loss of her parents, being put in a harem to be groomed to be the lover of a man who had no clue who she was.

All of these things were being used for a greater purpose and now, maybe for the first time, her life was starting to make sense and piece together. I can make a difference! I can take all the piercings and pains I've gone through and use them for something that I couldn't even imagine.

She was able to get into her sacred place and go deep with God because there was no place else to go. She was backed up against a wall and there was nowhere to turn but to HIM. Gracious as HE is; HE provided an answer for an entire nation.

Our lives don't just affect us, they affect those around us. When we are BRAVE enough to set aside our pain and dare to step into our greatness, so many others can benefit by that braveness. A new YOU will emerge that will lead you and others to a life that is filled with peace, strength, and purpose.

Run to Him. He is the only place, the only answer, and your strength in time of need.

Reach up to Him, He will receive you and bless you in ways you couldn't begin to imagine!

Novel Fun - Day 5

Shaken, not stirred.... 😮🧖

There she was, following the plan God had put in her heart. She was prudent enough to seek Him to get that blueprint that she needed to address a very pressing and devastating situation. She treaded lightly into that perceived darkness. She took her time; she listened and her heart was open to the Spirit of God to guide her into all truth. She couldn't chance leaving any of it to her own heart. She had to let that go and free herself from any obstructions that could cloud the clarity that was about to come.

She had to be free in heart and mind to receive what was necessary for now. Letting go of the past and what was behind her so that she could embrace the possibilities of the new day. She couldn't carry in her stuff from before, she had to leave it at the door. She had to enter freely so she could receive freely, so her future could change and be what HE wanted it to be, not what she wanted it to be.

Safety in the palace may have caused her to be complacent, but now there was a bigger cause to tend to. This was her time. She seized her day and moved forward with trepidation and peace, knowing all along that her God was with her, guiding her, strengthening her, and making all things work together for her good.

She knew there was an answer and if she continued in His strength instead of her own, she would receive it, and she did. She was obedient to the call, to the answer and the follow-through, and because of it, an entire nation was saved.

Who knows who you will save through your obedience and follow-through.

Novel Fun - Day 6

Three days! A lot can happen in three days! 

I find it interesting that Esther said she was going to fast for 3 days and come back with an answer... like if she did that, she would get results.

Esther expected God to speak to her. Maybe she had done that before or had been taught by Mordecai to do so. Her heritage was one of fasting and sackcloth to demonstrate that they were seeking God and were looking for direction. This act of fasting was also to help them focus on prayer and hearing from God, especially if they had something tantamount that they needed help with. There are many other examples of fasting coupled with prayer in the Word with answers and miracles following. ✳

The two, together, signified that you meant business. That you really needed help in this situation, and were expecting to hear from Him. When it comes to fasting itself, it depletes us of ourselves and brings us on a different level physically, spiritually, and emotionally.

Fasting and prayer became a way for me to quiet myself and put my body, soul, and spirit in a posture to hear on a physical and spiritual level.

What happens when you get to the end of yourself and you know you need to do something more because what you're currently doing is no longer holding water? Do you stop and ask God if He wants you to go deeper in this situation and really lean into Him? Jesus said that some things don't change but by prayer and fasting.

Posture yourself to hear Him. John leaned in to Jesus to hear what He had to say at the Last Supper because he sensed that something important was about to happen. Other prophets and greats of the Bible also positioned themselves to hear from God before proceeding on the path they thought they should be on. The Apostle Paul was on his own with the Lord for 14 years before being accepted by and eventually joining the other disciples in spreading the Good News.

Are you facing something you cannot handle on your own? Pray, fast, and lean into Him so He can guide you into all truth, like no one else can. 🙌

Novel Fun - Day 7

When you come out of a fast, it's usually in one of a few ways. After the third day, you can be tired, hungry, high, one, two, or maybe all three of these. The body goes into ketosis and most people, including myself, start to feel clearer, cleaner and more alert, and may even experience being on a higher spiritual plane. There's a strength that comes from within and that clarity causes you to do in His strength what you couldn't do on your own. There's a wisdom that comes because you've drawn closer to God and He's drawn closer to you.

It was as if something clicked and made sense from the fasting. Time without the comforts of the world and the noise of people around her gave her the clarity she needed to receive the plan to proceed. It may have come all at once or a little at a time as she took her steps forward. Esther may have also clearly seen the situation in ways she couldn't before.

It's important to get alone, apart from the voices of others, with only the voice of God. That is where the Truth comes. It doesn't come from fighting within; it comes from sitting still in His presence. That silence and fasting led to the answer.

Esther then got ready for the next step. She mustered the strength to put her life in God's hands and go to the King unannounced. She knew what to wear, when to go, and where to stand. Esther's fast was time well spent.

Have questions that don't have answers? Situations you're not sure how to handle? Draw near to Him and He will draw near to you. Ask for wisdom... He never denies wisdom to those who ask.

Novel Fun - Day 8

My fast has been fruitful, the Lord has visited me, answered my prayer, and given me strength to move in the direction in which I've been instructed. The plan is in my heart. My soul, mind, and spirit have been cleansed and, on His prompting, I will move forward.

I have prepared myself spiritually and now, I must prepare myself physically for the big ask. I will put on my best. From the top of my head to the bottom of my feet, I prepare myself to be well-received. I am the Queen, and I must walk in that authority mentally, physically, and emotionally, stepping into my call. At the same time, I am relying on the Lord to continue to prepare the path that is ahead of me.

I am confident the Lord has paved this path and my angels are going before me. I have prepared a meal for the King in faith. With trepidation and trembling within, strength and peace without, I make my way to the throne room. I gently peek my head in to see what's happening. Is today the right day to go in? Is it OK to proceed?

Oh! He's caught my eye! What is he thinking? Will I be banished like Vashti or maybe killed because I haven't been summoned? NO, I have to put my faith in God and let the doubt dissipate. Wait, I see him smiling. It's a good smile. He's putting out his scepter. I can go in, Praise God!

I am well-received! I will invite him to the dinner I have prepared, start with a good meal. Once he is appeased and comfortable, I can gain his ear, and the Lord will show me the next step. I must be careful to do as He has instructed so that the plan will go well for everyone. People's lives are at stake and I must put myself aside and put them first.

..... Esther, Queen of Persia and Medes

Novel Fun - Day 9

We're having a feast! She thought of the prior celebrations at the palace. Their decadence and how happy the King was during them. I'm sure the feasts were great times of gathering and festivity, as they were portrayed in the first chapter, debauchery aside. That's a story for another time.

Esther knew that the best way to get to her man's heart was through his stomach. She created an environment to help facilitate a good mood, prepare the King's heart, and provide an opportunity to present her plight and make her big ask.

By inviting Haman, she was keeping her enemy close. She built suspense by keeping her tongue and inviting them to a second banquet. I'm sure the King was up most of the night wondering what she had on her heart. And Haman, well, he was feeling really special being asked to go to another party with the King and Queen, which included bragging to all of his friends.

Esther most likely went home and began praying again, continuing to hear His voice and moving ahead with His plan.

Praying, listening, and taking action once we hear Him is so important. Being in constant fellowship, especially in times of great decision, is helpful to the success of how things will turn out. The more there is of Him and the less there is of us, the better our situations and lives will be.

Obedience is key in getting next steps. Like playing ball, the Lord will continue to fellowship with us as we fellowship with Him. He's always ready to draw nearer to us and help us with the most intimate and difficult of things. Big, small, the Lord handles them all… trust in Him with all your heart and lean into Him.

Novel Fun - Day 10

It's another feast day, yet it's different than the first. Today is the day that the Lord wants me to speak. He wants me to reveal the plan formed in the darkness and bring it to light. How do I tell the King that one of his trusted servants has betrayed him, and an entire nation, for his own selfish purposes, in order to carry out his hatred toward the people of God?

Not only that, I have to reveal to the King who I really am. That I am Hadassah, a Jew, born of Jewish parents and Jewish heritage. One of His chosen people, the apple of His eye. What if he rejects me and banishes me because of it and the entire nation perishes because of my omission?

I will trust the Lord that this is the proper time, and the wisdom in the hiding of my heritage was His plan all along. I will trust that the Lord has softened the King's heart towards me by the extending of his scepter to let me into the throne room and listen to what I have to say. After all, he was so delighted that he offered me anything, up to half his kingdom. He wanted me to speak my heart. Surely that means something.

Angels go before me! In trembling, I get closer to him. I am hoping he sees me as his wife, his beloved, his queen, and does not hold my heritage and the secret I'm about to reveal against me. I gently touch him, and in my loving voice, begin to explain my plight. He leans in and a tear comes to his eyes. That welling up turns to anger. He asks, "Who would do this to My Beloved and to her people?"

Thank you God that he truly has heard me, and that YOU have heard me and softened him. He really does see me and despite what he sees, what others may now see, he loves me. He loves me enough to rebuke his trusted "friend."

He's getting up to leave. Where is he going? He starts rubbing his head. I think he's angry and bewildered. And now, I see Haman. He knows he's in trouble and he's heading for me. What does he want from me? He's pulling at my dress. Why? Is he trying to get to me first and then make his way to the King?

Wait, the King is coming back. He's quickly making his way toward me. He's going to rescue me. He banishes the enemy and holds me close to him.

As he holds me, I feel that he's perplexed and doesn't know what to do because his love has rendered him slightly helpless. He knows that when a law is made, it cannot be changed. He doesn't want me or my people to die. He's so distraught he cannot think straight. He has forgotten that all he has to do is issue a new edict to override the other one and all will be well.

The new edict is issued. The enemy has been abolished and peace has been restored to the people. I am saved; they are saved.

The other countrymen knew our people all along and were confused when the first edict came out, and now they know why. It was all an evil plot!

The others are now in fear of us because we are many and are no longer considered the enemy or "those people." We are all in good-standing and we can now work in harmony toward a better future.

Thank you, God, for rescuing and preserving Your people. Thank you for choosing me in this time. Thank you for Your gracious, guiding hand. I will be forever grateful. THE END.

.....Esther, Queen of Persia and Medes

VI.

MY SOAP
STUDY JOURNAL

Chapter and Scripture Notes Using "SOAP"

*Y*ears ago, I learned how to use a Bible Study method called "SOAP".

This method aids in a deeper study of the Word, and promotes a higher rate of retention.

This is how the acronym "SOAP" is used to study the Bible....

S write the **S**cripture down
O make an **O**bservation of the Scripture
A find an **A**pplication of the Scripture to your life
P form a **P**rayer including the Scripture or with the Scripture in mind

Writing the **S**cripture, making an **O**bservation of that Scripture, finding a life **A**pplication and forming a **P**rayer to God helped me to see what I was reading in a different light and kept what I read in the forefront of my mind and heart.

I am sharing my personal notes with you. I hope you take the time and opportunity to create a journal of the same for yourself.

May my journey through this Book, at various times in my life, bless you and bring you closer to our Lord.

Esther 1:1-4

"Now it came to pass in the days of Ahasuerus (this was the Ahasuerus who reigned over one hundred and twenty-seven provinces, from India to Ethiopia), in those days when King Ahasuerus sat on the throne of his kingdom, which was in Shushan the citadel, that in the third year of his reign he made a feast for all his officials and servants—the powers of Persia and Media, the nobles, and the princes of the provinces being before him—when he showed the riches of his glorious kingdom and the splendor of his excellent majesty for many days, one hundred and eighty days in all."

Observation...

It is the Lord who gives us the power to get wealth (Deuteronomy 8:18) and we should not forget Him when He provides it for us.

We are to bless others with what He has provided for us, therefore ensuring that we are putting Him and His Kingdom first so others can be saved and glorify Him.

That is the true treasure that lasts that cannot be taken away.

Application...

Pray for wisdom on how to get more in order to give more to increase His Kingdom, so we ultimately steward our resources according to His divine will.

Prayer...

Lord God, help me to be diligent, prayerful, focused, and on task to what you have called me to do. Help me not to look to the right or to the left, but keep my eyes on You so I can please You and not man... to fulfill Your purpose and plans and not my own.

Esther 1:5-8

"And when these days were completed, the king made a feast lasting seven days for all the people who were present in Shushan the citadel, from great to small, in the court of the garden of the king's palace. There were white and blue linen curtains fastened with cords of fine linen and purple on silver rods and marble pillars; and the couches were of gold and silver on a mosaic pavement of alabaster, turquoise, and white and black marble. And they served drinks in golden vessels, each vessel being different from the other, with royal wine in abundance, according to the generosity of the king. In accordance with the law, the drinking was not compulsory; for so the king had ordered all the officers of his household, that they should do according to each man's pleasure."

Observation...

This passage shows a worldly view of riches.

Application...

Focus on Jesus and His Kingdom instead of earthly treasures and decorations.

God is in the details and He wants me to have His best, but not at the expense of my heart and soul.

Prayer...

Father, help me to attend to You, Your purposes, Your Word and not get caught up on the latest thing at the expense of my time. To focus on You, our intimacy and our relationship together, so my heart will always be free to draw near to You, with nothing between us.

Esther 1:9-12

"Queen Vashti also made a feast for the women in the royal palace which belonged to King Ahasuerus. On the seventh day, when the heart of the king was merry with wine, he commanded Mehuman, Biztha, Harbona, Bigtha, Abagtha, Zethar, and Carcas, seven eunuchs who served in the presence of King Ahasuerus, to bring Queen Vashti before the king, wearing her royal crown, in order to show her beauty to the people and the officials, for she was beautiful to behold. But Queen Vashti refused to come at the king's command brought by his eunuchs; therefore the king was furious, and his anger burned within him."

Observation...

The King had been making too many successively poor choices, which led to this last poor choice, which deeply angered him.

He took offense and let it fester and did not seek wise counsel, which caused the betrayal of his wife and the loss of the Queen, shaming her for his poor choices.

God used it all for His glory in the end, despite the King's poor choices.

Application...

My first thoughts and words are important when faced with the day-to-day choices and how I handle life.

Waiting to hear what God has to say, asking for wisdom and waiting for Him to answer will save everyone a lot of grief and potential shame.

Prayer...

Lord, help me to seek You continuously. To act according to my spirit and not my flesh, acting in love so that a multitude of sin can be covered by Your will being done.

Esther 1:13-18

"Then the king said to the wise men who understood the times (for this was the king's manner toward all who knew law and justice, those closest to him being Carshena, Shethar, Admatha, Tarshish, Meres, Marsena, and Memucan, the seven princes of Persia and Media, who had access to the king's presence, and who ranked highest in the kingdom): "What shall we do to Queen Vashti, according to law, because she did not obey the command of King Ahasuerus brought to her by the eunuchs?" And Memucan answered before the king and the princes: "Queen Vashti has not only wronged the king, but also all the princes, and all the people who are in all the provinces of King Ahasuerus. For the queen's behavior will become known to all women, so that they will despise their husbands in their eyes, when they report, 'King Ahasuerus commanded Queen Vashti to be brought in before him, but she did not come.' This very day the noble ladies of Persia and Media will say to all the king's officials that they have heard of the behavior of the queen. Thus there will be excessive contempt and wrath."

Observation...

The King was obtaining his wisdom from men who were most likely just as drunk as he was.

Despite the fact that they were rulers and part of his inner circle, they made a decision in the heat of the moment that caused many people pain.

Application...

It is best to look at all aspects of a thing when you are in your "right mind" and not intoxicated by anger or other emotions, which will most likely cloud your judgment and cause you to make a rash and imprudent decision.

Prayer...

Help me, Lord, to always seek You and Your Word first. Let that be the first place I go and not to the arm of the flesh, be it my own or someone else's.

Esther 1:19-22

"If it pleases the king, let a royal decree go out from him, and let it be recorded in the laws of the Persians and the Medes, so that it will not be altered, that Vashti shall come no more before King Ahasuerus; and let the king give her royal position to another who is better than she. When the king's decree which he will make is proclaimed throughout all his empire (for it is great), all wives will honor their husbands, both great and small." And the reply pleased the king and the princes, and the king did according to the word of Memucan. Then he sent letters to all the king's provinces, to each province in its own script, and to every people in their own language, that each man should be master in his own house, and speak in the language of his own people."

Observation...

The King was prideful and valued his office and the approval of others more than he valued his relationship with his wife (Vashti). He cared more about his public reputation being tarnished than the dignity and well-being of his wife. He came first, and he did not respect her, therefore she ultimately "disrespected" him.

Application...

Look at what is happening around me.

Assess the situations so that my decisions are made soberly, with good intentions, and in respect to those around me.

Prayer...

Prayers for my husband, that he continues to stay close to the Lord. That God would be his head so that his identity would come from His Word. That he would see himself as God sees him and would continue to love me as God loves him and His Church.

Esther 2:1-4

"After these things, when the wrath of King Ahasuerus subsided, he remembered Vashti, what she had done, and what had been decreed against her. Then the king's servants who attended him said: "Let beautiful young virgins be sought for the king; and let the king appoint officers in all the provinces of his kingdom, that they may gather all the beautiful young virgins to Shushan the citadel, into the women's quarters, under the custody of Hegai the king's eunuch, custodian of the women. And let beauty preparations be given them. Then let the young woman who pleases the king be queen instead of Vashti." This thing pleased the king, and he did so."

Observation...

The King was not making decisions with a sound mind. The Word circumspectly stands out. There is a careful consideration of all circumstances and a desire to avoid mistakes and bad consequences. (Ephesians 5:15)

Application...

I must look at all things full circle.

How will each decision I make, moment by moment, affect my husband, family, Christian walk, and my example to those around me?

What I do or do not do, even in the dark, always comes to light and will ultimately affect the outcome of my life and the lives of those around me, maybe even for generations to come.

Prayer...

Lord, help me to see the bigger picture, Your Kingdom and Your will for me, and how each decision I make affects it so that I can choose wisely and choose life, not death.

Esther 2:5-7

"In Shushan the citadel there was a certain Jew whose name was Mordecai the son of Jair, the son of Shimei, the son of Kish, a Benjamite. Kish had been carried away from Jerusalem with the captives who had been captured with Jeconiah king of Judah, whom Nebuchadnezzar the king of Babylon had carried away. And Mordecai had brought up Hadassah, that is, Esther, his uncle's daughter, for she had neither father nor mother. The young woman was lovely and beautiful. When her father and mother died, Mordecai took her as his own daughter."

Observation...

Take care of those who have less than us spiritually, emotionally, and monetarily, for this is God's will for our lives.

Application...

Make more time to visit and help others.

Prayer...

Lord, help me in wisdom to know where, when, and how I may help those around me with prayer and the resources you've given me.

Esther 2:8-11

"So it was, when the king's command and decree were heard, and when many young women were gathered at Shushan the citadel, under the custody of Hegai, that Esther also was taken to the king's palace, into the care of Hegai the custodian of the women. Now the young woman pleased him, and she obtained his favor; so he readily gave beauty preparations to her, besides her allowance. Then seven choice maidservants were provided for her from the king's palace, and he moved her and her maidservants to the best place in the house of the women. Esther had not revealed her people or family, for Mordecai had charged her not to reveal it. And every day Mordecai paced in front of the court of the women's quarters, to learn of Esther's welfare and what was happening to her."

Observation...

Obedience and submission to authority can and will bring great favor.

Application...

Resistance is pride. Knowing and obeying God's Word and the leading of His Spirit will lead to peace and harmony.

Prayer...

Lord, help me to bend like the tree to the wind of Your Spirit so that I may please You through my obedience and ultimate faith in Your Word coming to pass in my life. Help me to be pliable when I need to be and stand firm when I'm supposed to so Your will can be done in my life, and the lives of those You place in my path.

Esther 2:12-18

"Each young woman's turn came to go in to King Ahasuerus after she had completed twelve months' preparation, according to the regulations for the women, for thus were the days of their preparation apportioned: six months with oil of myrrh, and six months with perfumes and preparations for beautifying women. Thus prepared, each young woman went to the king, and she was given whatever she desired to take with her from the women's quarters to the king's palace. In the evening she went, and in the morning she returned to the second house of the women, to the custody of Shaashgaz, the king's eunuch who kept the concubines. She would not go in to the king again unless the king delighted in her and called for her by name.

Now when the turn came for Esther the daughter of Abihail the uncle of Mordecai, who had taken her as his daughter, to go in to the king, she requested nothing but what Hegai the king's eunuch, the custodian of the women, advised. And Esther obtained favor in the sight of all who saw her. So Esther was taken to King Ahasuerus, into his royal palace, in the tenth month, which is the month of Tebeth, in the seventh year of his reign. The king loved Esther more than all the other women, and she obtained grace and favor in his sight more than all the virgins; so he set the royal crown upon her head and made her queen instead of Vashti. Then the king made a great feast, the Feast of Esther, for all his officials and servants; and he proclaimed a holiday in the provinces and gave gifts according to the generosity of a king."

Observation...

There is a process of preparation before going before the King.

Obedience gave Esther beauty, grace, and favor.

Application...

Doing the will of God, obedience to His Word, and being in His presence will make all things beautiful.

Prayer...

Lord, help me to come boldly before Your throne so I can obtain Your favor, the only thing that matters. Help me to prepare myself to be in Your presence by putting aside everything but You and the desire to love You and praise You as You deserve, Oh King of Kings, Lord of Lords, and my most precious Ancient of Days. Glory and honor to You, my God and King!

Esther 2:19-23

"When virgins were gathered together a second time, Mordecai sat within the king's gate. Now Esther had not revealed her family and her people, just as Mordecai had charged her, for Esther obeyed the command of Mordecai as when she was brought up by him.

In those days, while Mordecai sat within the king's gate, two of the king's eunuchs, Bigthan and Teresh, doorkeepers, became furious and sought to lay hands on King Ahasuerus. So the matter became known to Mordecai, who told Queen Esther, and Esther informed the king in Mordecai's name. And when an inquiry was made into the matter, it was confirmed, and both were hanged on a gallows; and it was written in the book of the chronicles in the presence of the king."

Observation...

Listen to good counsel and be open to good instruction. Use wisdom in your affairs.

Application...

Know when to speak and when to keep silent.

Discern what to share and when to keep certain things secret, and avoid giving pearls to those who aren't ready to treasure them.

Prayer...

Psalm 19:14... Let the words of my mouth, and the thoughts of my heart be acceptable to You, oh Lord, my strength and my redeemer.

Esther 3:1-4

"After these things King Ahasuerus promoted Haman, the son of Hammedatha the Agagite, and advanced him and set his seat above all the princes who were with him. And all the king's servants who were within the king's gate bowed and paid homage to Haman, for so the king had commanded concerning him. But Mordecai would not bow or pay homage. Then the king's servants who were within the king's gate said to Mordecai, "Why do you transgress the king's command?" Now it happened, when they spoke to him daily and he would not listen to them, that they told it to Haman, to see whether Mordecai's words would stand; for Mordecai had told them that he was a Jew."

Observation...

As a child of God, I should only bow to Him... not to the circumstances around me, forgetting the Word and what God has already done and will do on my behalf. Nor should I bow to the people around me, seeking their approval or admonition.

Application...

Do the things of the Lord and only bend (bow) to His Word and ways.

Prayer...

Help me to stay focused on You. Let me not get distracted by things that will lead me away from Your presence and Your will for my day. Let me only bow to Your Word and Your wisdom.

Esther 3:5-6

"When Haman saw that Mordecai did not bow or pay him homage, Haman was filled with wrath. But he disdained to lay hands on Mordecai alone, for they had told him of the people of Mordecai. Instead, Haman sought to destroy all the Jews who were throughout the whole kingdom of Ahasuerus—the people of Mordecai."

Observation...

Emotions gone unchecked escalate to a higher level and can be a path to great destruction (like a city without walls is a man without self-control, Proverbs 25:28).

Keep your heart and spirit in check.

Application...

When you start feeling uneasy, get quiet with God.

Let His Spirit guide you into all truth, so you can direct your heart accordingly.

Trust the Lord to take care of the most frustrating and despairing situations that come your way.

Prayer...

Lord, help me to trust that nothing in this world, in my life and the lives of those around me is so impossible that it's beyond Your reach.

Help me to bring my concerns to You more quickly, trusting that You always concern yourself with everything that concerns me, and that all things will be made beautiful in their time. (Psalm 138:8, Ecclesiastes 3:11)

Esther 3:7-11

"In the first month, which is the month of Nisan, in the twelfth year of King Ahasuerus, they cast Pur (that is, the lot), before Haman to determine the day and the month, until it fell on the twelfth month, which is the month of Adar.

Then Haman said to King Ahasuerus, "There is a certain people scattered and dispersed among the people in all the provinces of your kingdom; their laws are different from all other people's, and they do not keep the king's laws. Therefore it is not fitting for the king to let them remain. If it pleases the king, let a decree be written that they be destroyed, and I will pay ten thousand talents of silver into the hands of those who do the work, to bring it into the king's treasuries."

So the king took his signet ring from his hand and gave it to Haman, the son of Hammedatha the Agagite, the enemy of the Jews. And the king said to Haman, "The money and the people are given to you, to do with them as seems good to you."

Observation...

The King was a bit hasty in handing over his authority without knowing all the facts.

Since so much was at stake, it was important to listen to all the details and get the proper facts, not just rely on hearsay.

We need to be careful with our words as they can bring blessing or cursing.

Application...

Seek the Lord and the Word first when faced with a situation before moving forward to solve the problem.

Prayer...

Lord, help me to seek You first. Help me to watch my first words. Help me to speak life and truth, blessing and not cursing in every situation.

Esther 3:12-13

"Then the king's scribes were called on the thirteenth day of the first month, and a decree was written according to all that Haman commanded—to the king's satraps, to the governors who were over each province, to the officials of all people, to every province according to its script, and to every people in their language. In the name of King Ahasuerus it was written, and sealed with the king's signet ring. And the letters were sent by couriers into all the king's provinces, to destroy, to kill, and to annihilate all the Jews, both young and old, little children and women, in one day, on the thirteenth day of the twelfth month, which is the month of Adar, and to plunder their possessions."

Observation...

There was a hatred for the people of God.

The people who have a hatred towards God's children will be punished.

Application...

Guard your heart, keep it in check.

Walk in love so that your anger does not give the enemy a foothold.

Prayer...

Lord, help me to understand that the enemy's hatred toward me is truly his anger toward You. And because I have righteousness with You through Jesus, I am protected from temporal and eternal destruction.

Esther 3:14-15

"A copy of the document was to be issued as law in every province, being published for all people, that they should be ready for that day. The couriers went out, hastened by the king's command; and the decree was proclaimed in Shushan the citadel. So the king and Haman sat down to drink, but the city of Shushan was perplexed."

Observation...

"Ready for that day."

Application...

How prepared am I for what happens, even when I'm warned ahead of time in the spirit or by others?

Am I "perplexed," clueless as to what is going on around me?

What best steps can I take when I'm faced with something so that I can prepare and have the best outcome?

Prayer...

Lord, help me to truly understand what You want, what Your will is for me and how to help those around me. Help me to act out of love through Your direction and not my own flesh.

Esther 4:1-3

"When Mordecai learned all that had happened, he tore his clothes and put on sackcloth and ashes, and went out into the midst of the city. He cried out with a loud and bitter cry. He went as far as the front of the king's gate, for no one might enter the king's gate clothed with sackcloth. And in every province where the king's command and decree arrived, there was great mourning among the Jews, with fasting, weeping, and wailing; and many lay in sackcloth and ashes."

Observation...

No one could enter the King's gate while wearing sackcloth. I am so grateful that no matter what state I am in, I can go boldly before the throne of God's grace and obtain the mercy I need for that specific moment.

I can go and say Hi to God and sit in His lap and hug Him whenever I want.

He won't despise me for going in just any old way. I can be clean, dirty, sad or broken, He will always let me in. He only looks at me through the Blood of Jesus, He is my scepter and my permission to go in.

I am able to enter in whenever I please because of His sacrifice.

Application...

I will go to the Lord bare, real, just like David and the prodigal son, seeking only Him, and allow Him to minister to me and to restore me.

Prayer...

Lord, You created me. You know me. Help me to come quickly before You, no matter the circumstances, to gain Your help in time of need and thank You for Your wisdom and mercy.

Esther 4:4-7

"So Esther's maids and eunuchs came and told her, and the queen was deeply distressed. Then she sent garments to clothe Mordecai and take his sackcloth away from him, but he would not accept them. Then Esther called Hathach, one of the king's eunuchs whom he had appointed to attend her, and she gave him a command concerning Mordecai, to learn what and why this was. So Hathach went out to Mordecai in the city square that was in front of the king's gate. And Mordecai told him all that had happened to him, and the sum of money that Haman had promised to pay into the king's treasuries to destroy the Jews."

Observation...

God always comforts us through His Word and the people and circumstances around us.

Application...

I will look to You, oh Lord, for my comfort and peace.

Prayer...

Thank You for being the God of ALL comfort. You are always with me in every situation. You never leave me or forsake me. I am truly grateful and I love You!!

Esther 4:8-11

"He also gave him a copy of the written decree for their destruction, which was given at Shushan, that he might show it to Esther and explain it to her, and that he might command her to go in to the king to make supplication to him and plead before him for her people. So Hathach returned and told Esther the words of Mordecai.

Then Esther spoke to Hathach, and gave him a command for Mordecai: "All the king's servants and the people of the king's provinces know that any man or woman who goes into the inner court to the king, who has not been called, he has but one law: put all to death, except the one to whom the king holds out the golden scepter, that he may live. Yet I myself have not been called to go in to the king these thirty days."

Observation...

There are laws in place, yet there is a special case that has created a sense of urgency to go before the throne to obtain mercy. In the Old

Testament, they were not able to go into the Holy of Holies.

In the New Testament, we are to go boldly before The Throne. The priests were the intercessors in the Old Testament. Jesus is now our priest and because of His blood, which makes us righteous, we can go freely and boldly before The Throne.

God is merciful and is moved by our contriteness of heart and our own faith in His Words.

Without faith, it's impossible to please Him.

Application...

I will go boldly before the throne of God because it has been made available to me and that's where my Daddy is.

I will go in faith of His Word that covers any situation or circumstances.

I will do the possible, and God will do the impossible.

Prayer...

Thank You, Father, that I always have a place to go. I am not alone and without hope in this world. You are my rock and my salvation. I will not be afraid.

Esther 4:12-14

"So they told Mordecai Esther's words.

And Mordecai told them to answer Esther: "Do not think in your heart that you will escape in the king's palace any more than all the other Jews. For if you remain completely silent at this time, relief and deliverance will arise for the Jews from another place, but you and your father's house will perish. Yet who knows whether you have come to the kingdom for such a time as this?"

Observation...

There is an appointed time of deliverance for God's people. If one summoned deliverer does not answer the call, God will send another because His desire is for all men to be saved.

Application...

I must not remain silent, in fear, feeling inadequate and without confidence.

God has a plan and a purpose and I must do His will unless I choose to perish, because He has people for me to reach, whose lives need to be changed.

Prayer...

Lord, I am truly feeling a sense of urgency today. Help me to stand in the confidence of Your Word and in the sure plan You have for me. Give me strength to walk out that plan. My desire is to please You and bring You glory. I want to fulfill that desire and help Your people.

Esther 4:15-17

"Then Esther told them to reply to Mordecai: "Go, gather all the Jews who are present in Shushan, and fast for me; neither eat nor drink for three days, night or day. My maids and I will fast likewise. And so I will go to the king, which is against the law; and if I perish, I perish!"

So Mordecai went his way and did according to all that Esther commanded him."

Observation...

The Lord will guide us.

His eyes see the beginning and the end and He will carry us through.

Application...

I will listen and wait for the Lord's guidance.

I will seek Him in all things.

Prayer...

Lord, help me to seek You in every decision so that I may do Your will. Your will leads to the path of righteousness, and I desire to obey. Help me remember Your written Word and Your specific words to me, so I may be quick to follow. I love You!!

Esther 5:1-3

"Now it happened on the third day that Esther put on her royal robes and stood in the inner court of the king's palace, across from the king's house, while the king sat on his royal throne in the royal house, facing the entrance of the house. So it was, when the king saw Queen Esther standing in the court, that she found favor in his sight, and the king held out to Esther the golden scepter that was in his hand. Then Esther went near and touched the top of the scepter.

And the king said to her, "What do you wish, Queen Esther? What is your request? It shall be given to you—up to half the kingdom!"

Observation...

A lot happens on the "3rd day".

Royal robes - hers, they belonged to her because she was queen.

We have our royal robes - the cloak of righteousness, it must be worn, it's ours, through Jesus.

Outer court, then inner court (we were outside, now we get to go inside because of Him).

Third day, because of Jesus, we have favor and can enter in. Matthew 9:20-22 If only I may touch the hem of His garment, I will be made well (whole).

Application...

Go boldly before Him.

He sees us in our royal robes because of Jesus's sacrifice on the cross.

That sacrifice is what covers us and gives us the favor we need to go before the Father and ask anything of Him.

Prayer...

Father, thank you for this awesome sacrifice that has given me access to a personal relationship with You. Thank You that You always see my royalty and not my sin, and that I have favor with You because of Jesus. I love Your Word. Your authority and royalty have been passed down to me. I am complete, accepted, and whole because of this awesome sacrifice. Thank You Father!!!

Esther 5:4-5

"So Esther answered, "If it pleases the king, let the king and Haman come today to the banquet that I have prepared for him."

Then the king said, "Bring Haman quickly, that he may do as Esther has said." So the king and Haman went to the banquet that Esther had prepared."

Observation...

Esther exercised wisdom and discernment and waited to explain her plight.

She acted with kindness, despite the gravity of the situation. The King only said her first name, didn't use her title. There was a familiarity, as there is with those who we love and have special relationships with.

God wants to grant our heart's desires and to fulfill the purposes He places on our hearts.

Application...

Use wisdom and wait for God to speak in each situation. Our first words matter.

Prayer...

Father, help me to be slow to anger and to continue to move without fear, even when the challenges seem bigger than me. No matter how quickly the fire is blazing or how loud the circumstances cry out, let me always hear You so I can be and do like Jesus... I say what my Father says and I do what my Father does. (John 5:19)

Esther 5:6-8

"At the banquet of wine the king said to Esther, "What is your petition? It shall be granted you. What is your request, up to half the kingdom? It shall be done!"

Then Esther answered and said, "My petition and request is this: If I have found favor in the sight of the king, and if it pleases the king to grant my petition and fulfill my request, then let the king and Haman come to the banquet which I will prepare for them, and tomorrow I will do as the king has said."

Observation...

The King is offering Esther a very big incentive to find out her request, to hear what was on her heart, and she considers the timing of the asking despite the imminent deadline.

It seems like he is a different man now. He's patient, kind and loving, not making hasty decisions, and cutting off his nose to spite his face. He is sober, maybe lacking in some sleep, but he's choosing love over imprudence and giving her an opportunity to express herself and reason out the situation, lifting his scepter in acceptance.

She is in a controlled, strategic hurry like holding your peace while the circumstance is screaming, but you've already brought it to God and you know He will come through and will show you how to resolve it.

Application...

Timing is everything, and God is always on time. He will show me when to sit and when to move. Listen, pray, then speak.

Prayer...

Father, help me to be more like Jesus, to listen, having prayed first, and then doing as You do and speaking as You speak. More of You and less of me Lord.

Esther 5:9-11

"So Haman went out that day joyful and with a glad heart; but when Haman saw Mordecai in the king's gate, and that he did not stand or tremble before him, he was filled with indignation against Mordecai. Nevertheless Haman restrained himself and went home, and he sent and called for his friends and his wife Zeresh. Then Haman told them of his great riches, the multitude of his children, everything in which the king had promoted him, and how he had advanced him above the officials and servants of the king."

Observation...

Haman was counting his chickens before they hatched. He was riding high on the coattail victory of his promotion, even though he got it by lying.

He soothed his anger and made himself feel better by looking at all he had amassed and bragging about it to others.

Despite all of his accomplishments, he was still letting the little things get to him and focusing on the minor instead of being grateful for the major.

Application...

Remember the Lord your God, for it is He who gives you the power to get wealth. (Deuteronomy 8:18)

Every good and perfect gift comes from above. (James 1:17) Everything I have should give glory to God because it is He that has provided for my needs.

Prayer...

Lord, help me to always remember You, in times of famine and riches. Let me come to You in the same frequency in times of plenty as I do in desperate times of famine. Let me remember You, and always thank You, especially when my prayers have been answered, and turn to the answered prayer as if it was You in my presence.

Esther 5:12-14

"Moreover Haman said, "Besides, Queen Esther invited no one but me to come in with the king to the banquet that she prepared; and tomorrow I am again invited by her, along with the king. Yet all this avails me nothing, so long as I see Mordecai the Jew sitting at the king's gate."

Then his wife Zeresh and all his friends said to him, "Let a gallows be made, fifty cubits high, and in the morning suggest to the king that Mordecai be hanged on it; then go merrily with the king to the banquet."

And the thing pleased Haman; so he had the gallows made."

Observation...

Haman was in a prestigious position, had special privileges and yet, he was unsatisfied, letting the little foxes get to him. The more evil you let in, the more of a foothold is given to the enemy and the further off the path of God we go.

Application...

Walk in love and do not let the little things distract you from God's Word and His ultimate plan and will for your life. Take a five minute time out before dealing with anything. The thoughts may come, but I don't have to dwell on them or act out on them.

Prayer...

Lord, help me not to lose sight of Your voice in my heart. Let it be the beacon to my feet, so I follow the path you have for me because only Your path brings truth and blessing. I love You and I am humbled and grateful for Your great sacrifice of redemption so I can eternally enjoy fellowship with You.

Esther 6:1-3

"That night the king could not sleep. So one was commanded to bring the book of the records of the chronicles; and they were read before the king. And it was found written that Mordecai had told of Bigthana and Teresh, two of the king's eunuchs, the doorkeepers who had sought to lay hands on King Ahasuerus. Then the king said, "What honor or dignity has been bestowed on Mordecai for this?"

And the king's servants who attended him said, "Nothing has been done for him."

Observation...

The Lord uses even our lack of sleep for his good purposes. A good deed or kind action never goes unnoticed or un-rewarded by God.

Right words are a pleasure to hear.

Application...

Seek to do right by those around you and those that God has put in your path. You may be entertaining angels. Be kind, loving, and gentle with your words.

Prayer...

Father, help me to be wise in speech and action, acting according to Your Word, and in Your Spirit, and not in my flesh.

Esther 6:4-6

"So the king said, "Who is in the court?" Now Haman had just entered the outer court of the king's palace to suggest that the king hang Mordecai on the gallows that he had prepared for him.

The king's servants said to him, "Haman is there, standing in the court."

And the king said, "Let him come in."

So Haman came in, and the king asked him, "What shall be done for the man whom the king delights to honor?"

Now Haman thought in his heart, "Whom would the king delight to honor more than me?"

Observation...

God has our blessing in mind.

He sees the things we do in secret and seeks to reward us. The enemy seeks our destruction with a haughty heart, always pointing to our sins, magnifying what is negative and disregarding what is of good report, so he gets more credit. But God sees all through the eyes of Jesus, whose sacrifice paid for those sins, and the punishment is reversed.

What the enemy meant for our distraction and destruction; God will turn for our good.

Application...

Remember that no matter what happens, I will always be judged through the sacrifice of Jesus and that the wicked one cannot touch me.

God's plan is for good, for hope, and an expected end, and it's not the end the enemy has planned, it's the one God has for me.

Prayer...

I love you Lord and the fact that despite all; I am forgiven. You have the Words of everlasting life. You are my hope, strength, shield, and fortress.

Esther 6:7-9

"And Haman answered the king, "For the man whom the king delights to honor, let a royal robe be brought which the king has worn, and a horse on which the king has ridden, which has a royal crest placed on its head. Then let this robe and horse be delivered to the hand of one of the king's most noble princes, that he may array the man whom the king delights to honor. Then parade him on horseback through the city square, and proclaim before him: 'Thus shall it be done to the man whom the king delights to honor!' "

Observation...

Haman thought more highly of himself than the King, and the very thing he wanted for himself was done for his enemy.

The enemy wants our destruction, but the revelation is that he will be destroyed in the end, and we will be with our Father, King, and Wonderful Counselor.

Application...

Remember that the Lord has a plan for me. I have to seek my wise and wonderful Counselor for that plan, and allow Him to guide me into all truth, show me things to come, and then obey Him.

Prayer...

Lord, help me not to get ahead of myself, but also to keep up and move according to Your plan so You can raise me up and place me on solid ground.

Esther 6:10-11

"Then the king said to Haman, "Hurry, take the robe and the horse, as you have suggested, and do so for Mordecai the Jew who sits within the king's gate! Leave nothing undone of all that you have spoken."

So Haman took the robe and the horse, arrayed Mordecai and led him on horseback through the city square, and proclaimed before him, "Thus shall it be done to the man whom the king delights to honor!"

Observation...

Do all things unto God.

He sees all and in doing so, He will reward in due season what is done with the right heart.

Application...

I must live my life only for God.

Everything I do is for Him.

He will exalt me and put me in places where men cannot touch me because of His love, protection and promises... they are always with me.

Prayer...

Help me, oh God, not to be weary in well doing, to display the love you've given me for others. Catapult me to where You know I need to be. Your thoughts are not mine, and Your will is always best.

Esther 6:12-14

"Afterward Mordecai went back to the king's gate. But Haman hurried to his house, mourning and with his head covered. When Haman told his wife Zeresh and all his friends everything that had happened to him, his wise men and his wife Zeresh said to him, "If Mordecai, before whom you have begun to fall, is of Jewish descent, you will not prevail against him but will surely fall before him.""

While they were still talking with him, the king's eunuchs came, and hastened to bring Haman to the banquet which Esther had prepared."

Observation...

Even the heathen knows the blessings that are on the people of God. God always blesses His people, no matter what!

Application...

Remember that the Lord God is for me.

Only the enemy wants to kill us, steal our lives and our things, destroy what we love, and thwart our future.

I have favor because of God's grace and Jesus's sacrifice. I have been grafted into the Kingdom of God.

Prayer…

Help me to remember that I belong to You and that all of my days are ordained by You. There is nothing missing, lacking, or broken in my life. I have everything I need and the enemy only has the power I'll give him through my thoughts, words, and deeds. More of You and less of me, so the gap can be bridged, and the enemy squashed.

Esther 7:1-2

"So the king and Haman went to dine with Queen Esther. And on the second day, at the banquet of wine, the king again said to Esther, "What is your petition, Queen Esther? It shall be granted you. And what is your request, up to half the kingdom? It shall be done!"

Observation...

It seems as if Esther was waiting for God's prompting to make a request now.

Maybe she was waiting for wisdom and words so it would be the Lord and not her own flesh that would answer for the King's heart to be truly ready to hear her request and grant it.

Application...

I don't have to wait for an "appropriate time" to go before God's throne.

I can go without anxiousness, knowing that He hears me, thank Him for what He's already done, and for the answer to my current request.

Prayer...

Thank You that I can come at any time with any request and place it before You. Thank You, that You concern yourself with everything that concerns me, that You never sleep or slumber, and are always working things together for my good. I love you my Friend, my Father, and my God.

Esther 7:3-4

"Then Queen Esther answered and said, "If I have found favor in your sight, O king, and if it pleases the king, let my life be given me at my petition, and my people at my request. For we have been sold, my people and I, to be destroyed, to be killed, and to be annihilated. Had we been sold as male and female slaves, I would have held my tongue, although the enemy could never compensate for the king's loss."

Observation...

Slavery sometimes seems better than death and annihilation in the history of God's people.

Jesus's sacrifice is the only payment for our freedom.

The enemy knows who we are, and has been plotting our destruction forever. However, Jesus saved us from the destruction and came to give us life, and life more abundantly. (John 10:10)

Application...

I am redeemed from the curse and a life of destruction.

God has provided an opportunity for abundant life.

Remember the sacrifice in the heart of the battle, which belongs to God, and that the final outcome is always victory because of Jesus's purchase.

Prayer...

I am so grateful for You and to You. Help me to see what the abundant life is that You died to provide for me, and help me to capture that vision and run with it no matter what day, hour, or circumstance.

Esther 7:5-6

"So King Ahasuerus answered and said to Queen Esther, "Who is he, and where is he, who would dare presume in his heart to do such a thing?"

And Esther said, "The adversary and enemy is this wicked Haman!"

So Haman was terrified before the king and queen."

Observation...

An enemy... a person who is actively opposed or hostile to someone or something.

An adversary... a person who fights against or opposes another... against or contrary to someone.

The enemy/adversary is so evil that Esther used the word twice. He's hostile, he hates, opposes, and wants to fight against/annihilate his enemy.

Application...

Remember, the enemy can only go so far before the Lord steps in, just like in Job's story.

God always wants what's best for me.

I am the apple of His eye, and no harm will come to me.

Prayer...

Lord, help me to remember when I am under attack and faced with adversity, that You have already fought for me and Your sacrifice and Your Word have made me a champion no matter what the enemy sends my way. You even save me from myself!

Esther 7:7-8

"Then the king arose in his wrath from the banquet of wine and went into the palace garden; but Haman stood before Queen Esther, pleading for his life, for he saw that evil was determined against him by the king. When the king returned from the palace garden to the place of the banquet of wine, Haman had fallen across the couch where Esther was. Then the king said, "Will he also assault the queen while I am in the house?"

As the word left the king's mouth, they covered Haman's face."

Observation...

The King was so angered by the news he had just heard that he walked away for a minute.

When he came back, he was still angry and may not have seen the situation in its proper light, recognizing the plot.

Haman is so desperate for his life to be spared that he starts pleading with the Queen and seems to be attacking her, pulling on her to get his plight heard.

The Lord made all things? 😆

Application...

Walk away physically or in spirit, if necessary, when faced with the situation in order to gain wisdom, perspective and guidance from God, not from my flesh.

Do not act or speak quickly... next and first words should be from God and His Word, not from my flesh, so that I do not aggravate the situation, or hurt other people's feelings.

Prayer...

Lord, help me to bring everything to You first. You always have the answer and only Your Word is truth (You have the words of everlasting life). There is something in Your Word for all of life's happenings.

Esther 7:9-10

"Now Harbonah, one of the eunuchs, said to the king, "Look! The gallows, fifty cubits high, which Haman made for Mordecai, who spoke good on the king's behalf, is standing at the house of Haman."

Then the king said, "Hang him on it!"

So they hanged Haman on the gallows that he had prepared for Mordecai. Then the king's wrath subsided."

Observation...

The plans of Haman that were "secret" came to light.

The evil in his heart was seen in public because he never did anything to keep it in check and deal with it in secret.

The evil he planned for someone else rolled back on him.

Our sins have been rolled onto Jesus, and when He was hung and died, our belief and profession of Him gave us life.

God the Father's wrath on humanity's sin subsided with Jesus's sacrifice on the cross.

Application...

Keep my heart with all diligence.

Do not let things go unchecked do not let anything go on for an extended period of time without resolution through God's Word.

Do not let the sun go down on your anger.

Remember Jesus's sacrifice and that I am right with God because of it.

Prayer...

Father, thank You for counting me as one of your children. I am not an orphan and I'm not alone. You are always there for me, and I have direct access to You, the walls are down because of Jesus.

Esther 8:1-10

"On that day King Ahasuerus gave Queen Esther the house of Haman, the enemy of the Jews. And Mordecai came before the king, for Esther had told how he was related to her. So the king took off his signet ring, which he had taken from Haman, and gave it to Mordecai; and Esther appointed Mordecai over the house of Haman.

Now Esther spoke again to the king, fell down at his feet, and implored him with tears to counteract the evil of Haman the Agagite, and the scheme which he had devised against the Jews. And the king held out the golden scepter toward Esther. So Esther arose and stood before the king, and said, "If it pleases the king, and if I have found favor in his sight and the thing seems right to the king and I am pleasing in his eyes, let it be written to revoke the letters devised by Haman, the son of Hammedatha the Agagite, which he wrote to annihilate the Jews who are in all the king's provinces. For how can I endure to see the evil that will come to my people? Or how can I endure to see the destruction of my countrymen?"

Then King Ahasuerus said to Queen Esther and Mordecai the Jew, "Indeed, I have given Esther the house of Haman, and they have hanged him on the gallows because he tried to lay his hand on the Jews. You yourselves write a decree concerning the Jews, as you please, in the king's name, and seal it with the king's signet ring; for whatever is written in the king's name and sealed with the king's signet ring no one can revoke."

So the king's scribes were called at that time, in the third month, which is the month of Sivan, on the twenty-third day; and it was written, according to all that Mordecai commanded, to the Jews, the satraps, the governors, and the princes of the provinces from India to Ethiopia, one hundred and twenty-seven provinces in all, to every province in its own script, to every people in their own language, and to the Jews in their own script and language. And he wrote in the name of King Ahasuerus, sealed it with the king's signet ring, and sent letters by couriers on horseback, riding on royal horses bred from swift steeds."

Observation...

Esther went before the King twice, where he had to put up his scepter.

Parallel in the day of kings and for us because of Jesus...

A decree can be spoken on the King's behalf, in His Name, because of the authority He's given us and it has to be carried out because of the authority behind it and the declaration that's made. Jesus was the signet ring that put the laws of the Word into action. The authority He lavishes on us makes us kings and priests and we can declare His Word to change situations and bring peace to them.

Application...

The Lord gives me access, no matter what.

I can speak my heart to Him.

Because of Jesus's power of attorney given to me, I can speak a thing, and it will come to pass. (Job 22:28).

My words are important, they go out into the universe and create life.

What I say truly matters and will come to pass.

Prayer...

Lord, help me to remember Your love and compassion for me. No matter the circumstance, I can always come before You and You never turn Your face from me.

Esther 8:11-17

"By these letters the king permitted the Jews who were in every city to gather together and protect their lives—to destroy, kill, and annihilate all the forces of any people or province that would assault them, both little children and women, and to plunder their possessions, on one day in all the provinces of King Ahasuerus, on the thirteenth day of the twelfth month, which is the month of Adar. A copy of the document was to be issued as a decree in every province and published for all people, so that the Jews would be ready on that day to avenge themselves on their enemies. The couriers who rode on royal horses went out, hastened and pressed on by the king's command. And the decree was issued in Shushan the citadel.

So Mordecai went out from the presence of the king in royal apparel of blue and white, with a great crown of gold and a garment of fine linen and purple; and the city of Shushan rejoiced and was glad. The Jews had light and gladness, joy and honor. And in every province and city, wherever the king's command and decree came, the Jews had joy and gladness, a feast and a holiday. Then many of the people of the land became Jews, because fear of the Jews fell upon them."

Observation...

This is a precursor to the New Testament.

A decree published for all the provinces.

A copy issued so all could believe and be saved.

Application...

God's Word always prevails.
We have overcome the enemy!
Decree it, believe it, and you will be saved.

Prayer...

Thank you for Your Word and my salvation through Jesus. For going ahead and planning salvation for me when the enemy sought our destruction in the garden. Your love and provision have no bounds.

Esther 9:1-10

"Now in the twelfth month, that is, the month of Adar, on the thirteenth day, the time came for the king's command and his decree to be executed. On the day that the enemies of the Jews had hoped to overpower them, the opposite occurred, in that the Jews themselves overpowered those who hated them. The Jews gathered together in their cities throughout all the provinces of King Ahasuerus to lay hands on those who sought their harm. And no one could withstand them, because fear of them fell upon all people. And all the officials of the provinces, the satraps, the governors, and all those doing the king's work, helped the Jews, because the fear of Mordecai fell upon them. For Mordecai was great in the king's palace, and his fame spread throughout all the provinces; for this man Mordecai became increasingly prominent. Thus the Jews defeated all their enemies with the stroke of the sword, with slaughter and destruction, and did what they pleased with those who hated them.

And in Shushan the citadel the Jews killed and destroyed five hundred men. Also Parshandatha, Dalphon, Aspatha, Poratha, Adalia, Aridatha, Parmashta, Arisai, Aridai, and Vajezatha—the ten sons of Haman the son of Hammedatha, the enemy of the Jews—they killed; but they did not lay a hand on the plunder."

Observation...

On crucifixion day, our enemy thought he had gotten the best of Jesus, but His death, as decreed in the Word, was used as a sacrifice for our salvation.

Defeated their enemies with the sword of God's Word.

Application...

A great sacrifice led to my victory.

I am victorious against all of my enemies because Jesus went before me and made it so.

Prayer...

Thank you, Lord, that You are for me, that You came for my abundant life and to remove destruction and death from me.

Esther 9:11-22

"Now in the twelfth month, that is, the month of Adar, on the thirteenth day, the time came for the king's command and his decree to be executed. On the day that the enemies of the Jews had hoped to overpower them, the opposite occurred, in that the Jews themselves overpowered those who hated them. The Jews gathered together in their cities throughout all the provinces of King Ahasuerus to lay hands on those who sought their harm. And no one could withstand them, because fear of them fell upon all people. And all the officials of the provinces, the satraps, the governors, and all those doing the king's work, helped the Jews, because the fear of Mordecai fell upon them. For Mordecai was great in the king's palace, and his fame spread throughout all the provinces; for this man Mordecai became increasingly prominent. Thus the Jews defeated all their enemies with the stroke of the sword, with slaughter and destruction, and did what they pleased with those who hated them.

And in Shushan the citadel the Jews killed and destroyed five hundred men. Also Parshandatha, Dalphon, Aspatha, Poratha, Adalia, Aridatha, Parmashta, Arisai, Aridai, and Vajezatha—the ten sons of Haman the son of Hammedatha, the enemy of the Jews—they killed; but they did not lay a hand on the plunder.

On that day the number of those who were killed in Shushan the citadel was brought to the king. And the king said to Queen Esther, "The Jews have killed and destroyed five hundred men in Shushan the citadel, and the ten sons of Haman. What have they done in the rest of the king's provinces? Now what is your petition? It shall be granted to you. Or what is your further request? It shall be done."

Then Esther said, "If it pleases the king, let it be granted to the Jews who are in Shushan to do again tomorrow according to today's decree, and let Haman's ten sons be hanged on the gallows."

So the king commanded this to be done; the decree was issued in Shushan, and they hanged Haman's ten sons.

And the Jews who were in Shushan gathered together again on the fourteenth day of the month of Adar and killed three hundred men at Shushan; but they did not lay a hand on the plunder.

The remainder of the Jews in the king's provinces gathered together and protected their lives, had rest from their enemies, and killed seventy-five thousand of their enemies; but they did not lay a hand on the plunder. This was on the thirteenth day of the month of Adar. And on the fourteenth of the month they rested and made it a day of feasting and gladness.

The Feast of Purim

But the Jews who were at Shushan assembled together on the thirteenth day, as well as on the fourteenth; and on the fifteenth of the month they rested, and made it a day of feasting and gladness. Therefore the Jews of the villages who dwelt in the unwalled towns celebrated the fourteenth day of the month of Adar with gladness and feasting, as a holiday, and for sending presents to one another.

And Mordecai wrote these things and sent letters to all the Jews, near and far, who were in all the provinces of King Ahasuerus, to establish among them that they should celebrate yearly the fourteenth and fifteenth days of the month of Adar, as the days on which the Jews had rest from their enemies, as the month which was turned from sorrow to joy for them, and from mourning to a holiday; that they should make them days of feasting and joy, of sending presents to one another and gifts to the poor."

Observation...

Once again, the King asks Esther what her desires are (after the first desire was unspoken).

None of the plunder was touched.

There was a celebration after the victory to mark it as a remembrance of what had happened as their lives were spared.

They had rest from their enemies.

Application...

Bring your requests to God, knowing He always hears us. (John 11:42)

Remember His desire for me is ultimate victory from my enemies.

Give Him glory and remember the victories He gives me.

I overcome by the Blood of The Lamb and the words of my testimony. (Revelation 12:11).

The enemy needs to be reminded that I know that I am a winner according to God.

Prayer...

Thank You Lord for giving me the desires of my heart. For true victory over my enemy. I will not forget You and what You have done for me.

Esther 9:23-10:3

"So the Jews accepted the custom which they had begun, as Mordecai had written to them, because Haman, the son of Hammedatha the Agagite, the enemy of all the Jews, had plotted against the Jews to annihilate them, and had cast Pur (that is, the lot), to consume them and destroy them; but when Esther came before the king, he commanded by letter that this wicked plot which Haman had devised against the Jews should return on his own head, and that he and his sons should be hanged on the gallows.

So they called these days Purim, after the name Pur. Therefore, because of all the words of this letter, what they had seen concerning this matter, and what had happened to them, the Jews established and imposed it upon themselves and their descendants and all who would join them, that without fail they should celebrate these two days every year, according to the written instructions and according to the prescribed time, that these days should be remembered and kept throughout every generation, every family, every province, and every city, that these days of Purim should not fail to be observed among the Jews, and that the memory of them should not perish among their descendants.

Then Queen Esther, the daughter of Abihail, with Mordecai the Jew, wrote with full authority to confirm this second letter about Purim. And Mordecai sent letters to all the Jews, to the one hundred and twenty-seven provinces of the kingdom of Ahasuerus, with words of peace and truth, to confirm these days of Purim at their appointed time, as Mordecai the Jew and Queen Esther had prescribed for them, and as they had decreed for themselves and their descendants concerning matters of their fasting and lamenting. So the decree of Esther confirmed these matters of Purim, and it was written in the book.

And King Ahasuerus imposed tribute on the land and on the islands of the sea. Now all the acts of his power and his might, and the account of the greatness of Mordecai, to which the king advanced him, are they not written in the book of the chronicles of the kings of Media and

Persia? For Mordecai the Jew was second to King Ahasuerus, and was great among the Jews and well received by the multitude of his brethren, seeking the good of his people and speaking peace to all his countrymen."

Observation...

The Lord reminds us to feast in order to celebrate the milestones of our lives where He has given us breakthrough, lest we forget what He has done and despair in the next attack.

Glory is given to God through celebration and remembrance.

Application...

Make a gratitude journal and/or jar so that I remember the little things that the Lord does that lead to big things in my life.

Be mindful of His winks.

Not one thing is to be spared.

His goodness is to be remembered and revered, counted over to Him as kisses to His face, and hugs to His neck.

Prayer...

Father, let me always remember what You have taken me through. Let me remember the victories so I can use them as stones in the face of the enemy when he comes to give me grief. Let Your goodness to me be a reminder to him of who he's messing with so that he leaves as he left Jesus in the desert. It is written! (Matthew 4:3-4)

VII.

THE FINALE

Waiting Well
Listen, Rest,
and Obey

The soul pain that comes from trying to align ourselves with the wrong people can cost us years of our lives and potentially send us down heart-wrenching paths.

During my study of Esther, the Lord showed me how important it is to wait for "the one" that He has for us. God's plan for our lives encompasses everything that is dear to our hearts, and that includes our future mates.

I didn't wait well during the early years of my life. I got into relationships that were not healthy for me. I ran to them to escape things that were happening in my life and to feel loved and validated. I gave away pieces of myself that later hurt me physically, spiritually, and emotionally.

The healing process was long, and it nearly crushed me.

Like a lost soul wandering the earth, I drifted through life in emotional pain for years, making one poor decision after another. I lived life, but it wasn't peaceful or fulfilling. I packed it with activities and people in attempts to soothe and heal the hole in my heart.

Once I truly accepted Christ within me and began having a personal relationship with Him, seeking Him on a deep and daily basis, I started praying for the mate He wanted for me. The Lord had me make a list of specific things that I wanted in a husband, and I tucked it away.

I was "waiting for God" to bring a certain person for me. One night, I realized that I was making this thing into an idol. I went into my spare room, which had become my prayer sanctuary. I had two roommates who had stayed in that room and later, each moved out to get married. I affectionately called it my Bridal Suite. I had even hung my flowers from one of the weddings on my floor lamp. A few light-colored roses with baby's breath held together by a beautiful white mesh bow, hanging down as a symbol that two went before me, and prayerfully, I was next.

I walked into the inner sanctum to meet my King. I threw myself on the bed and asked Him for forgiveness for having put someone, a certain person, and something, the desire to have a mate, before Him.

I closed my eyes, and I felt His presence. I saw a vision of Him coming toward me. He was a large white and bright light, full of peace, with an indescribable loving energy. He came closer to me and hugged me. I could feel Him and His warm love, heart to heart, chest to chest. His cheek was against mine, and as He held me, He gently whispered to me… "finally, there is nothing between you and Me."

The chains around me and the pains inside me from years of bondage disintegrated and fell off, like ashes to the floor. That miraculous experience has become a treasured memory, and that feeling has manifested many other times while seeking His presence, especially in the most devastating of periods in my life.

Anything that we put before God becomes an idol. God is a jealous God. His desire is that not one person or thing is in first place, where He should be. When we put something else first, it distances us from Him, and we're not free to be our true selves with Him because there's something between us.

Whatever you are going through, God can help you through it. No one person, friend, family member or mate should ever take more precedence over our relationship with our Father.

We must be wise and true to our relationship with God. The world can sometimes be a sad and lonely place. When we're going through things, we can turn within ourselves and have a false sense of reality. Having safe people to confide in can save our lives from a path of destruction.

Ask yourself, who or what am I trying to escape? Who or what am I escaping to so that I don't have to deal with this situation? Why do I want to run from this? Is it because it's truth and I am in a state of rebellion and want what I want so I have no desire to listen? Do I think I know better than those who have walked before me?

Maybe we want to escape our parents because we think they are not treating us fairly. Or because we see how other parents are treating their children and we seem different. Parents are people too. They are our role models and we look up to them. However, now that I'm older, I realize that they too had their own things going on. They had their own experiences and insecurities to deal with, and they tried to parent us the best way they knew how. It wasn't always perfect, especially when they tried to protect us from the things of the world, but at least they were trying.

If we keep that in mind, it will be easier when they tell us something that requires a grain of salt to swallow.

Getting into relationships that are unhealthy just because we want to feel loved and accepted will only burn us in the end. There are signs of a person's true nature (especially potential mates) all around us. Lack of kindness and sudden outbursts that may seem random but are really true patterns of their demeanor and behavior;

are things to look out for. The way people treat others is the way they are eventually going to treat us.

Many people are walking around broken, but if they're looking for ways to heal that brokenness, and want to be better for themselves and others, then that is something to consider. However, overlooking signs of malfeasance when it's right in front of your face can lead to a painful relationship and, most likely, a painful life. Just because you think that person is going to change at some point doesn't mean it will happen.

Please wait for the one that God has for you. It will be better than any other experience you have had in life. Knowing that God truly brought that person to you, and that you waited for God, and relied on Him instead of yourself to make the decision, will give you hope on days when relationships become truly "human" and you begin to wonder what it's all about.

Please do not hang on to the first person who shows you the faintest sign of affection or validation. Step back and try to see it through the eyes of others and have them help you. Trusted family members and friends know you and they can help you determine what path is best for you.

I'm not saying that you go against what you feel in your heart, but at least listen to what others are saying and, above all, listen to the promptings of the Holy Spirit. He is your True North.

Please don't run away within yourself or to that person just because something else is shoving you in a direction that leaves you hopeless, and you think "this is it" (the one).

We can all run to unhealthy things to deal with life, but trust me, this is not like eating a donut that you weren't supposed to because you are on a diet. This is a matter that can potentially harm you, and maybe others, for life.

Do you learn a lesson and come out better? Maybe so, but why put yourself in a position to learn a lesson the hard way and be scarred for life? Learn from the words and experiences of others in each situation, and for as many life issues as you can.

There is power and wisdom that comes from making our own mistakes. However, there is greater power in being wise and waiting, learning from the advice and experiences of others.

There are signs everywhere. Look for them. The Holy Spirit is always talking and no man or woman is worth your relationship with God or years of healing and regret.

I waited! My story's up next.

You Can't Hurry Love
The Story of Us

The fruit, benefits and blessings that come from obeying God are exponential. Many years ago, I met a wonderful man.

There are so many little God-wink moments in the story of us, so to give you hope, and some amusing details, this is how I waited for my mate...

First, let me start off by saying that I didn't feel like I waited very well. I had to learn the hard way what it meant to wait on God. And not just wait, but trust.

It's so easy to say "God, I trust you" and then take it back when things don't seem to be going your way. That was my walk, a series of short bursts of faith.

I would trust, and then I would fall. I would trust and then I'd stop for a bit because it all seemed so bizarre, and then I'd get back on my path of faith.

There are so many distractions and things that happen in life that make us think and wonder if it's really God. Does He hear my prayers? Does He care about my heart and my life?

Once I truly gave my heart to God, my life started going in a positive direction. I had a come to Jesus moment when my dream, as I knew it, shattered.

Reality hit me in the face and I had to come to terms with the fact that what I had been believing to be true, instead, had gone in the wrong direction. Now, there had to be a new truth, God's truth, which is *the* only truth.

I felt led to make a list of the things that I was looking for in a husband. This was a desire to put before the Lord and to help guide me in times when I might want to wane from what I had written, and what God had put on my heart that was for me. Like why are you eating an apple when you've asked Him for an orange?

The Word says that without vision we perish. We have to write our visions down in order to run with them. Once I had that special and miraculous encounter with Him, and I saw that vision with my spiritual eyes, I let everything else go. I wasn't going to be out there searching.

I originally met my husband through work. My friend introduced me to one of our business associates that I had not met. We hit it off and spent hours talking. We realized how much we had in common and how close our families were. Then, just as I was about to leave, he walked in.

We all hung out and shared many special things together. We talked about deep personal, emotional, and spiritual experiences, and all became very close. Eventually we moved and got separated, and my friend, his wife, passed away.

My life was busy. I was very involved in church, various groups, and my business. One Sunday, very early in the morning, while driving home after doing makeup for a bride sailing on a cruise ship, I realized I hadn't answered a phone message I'd received from a friend. You know… you get a call, listen to the message, delete it, and then forget to respond?

I called my friend and apologized. I asked how she was doing and she said she was still in the state and that she was on her way to the mall. I lived close to that mall, and we decided to meet for lunch. My now husband happened to be on that ride-along and that day we reconnected. I always looked at him as my friend's husband and big brother, so I didn't really have any romantic feelings towards him.

We started meeting every so often just to catch up on life. One day, when we met for dinner, we crossed an emotional line as the casual hug we greeted each other with lingered and felt extra-special. It was weird, and later that night, I had a vision of us being in some kind of ministry. This, after he said that he didn't know what God wanted from his life. The drive home from that encounter was different, and something weird had started in my heart and mind.

I had to let it go and let God work on things because I was seeing signs I wasn't sure of. This time, I wanted it to be God bringing it and not me pulling it in and making it happen.

On one particular night, I couldn't take the emotional pain. While lying on my bed, I just rolled to my side and said Lord, "please help me… here, take my heart" and I spiritually saw and felt it plop out of my chest and onto the bed, "I can't take it anymore please take it in your hands." I literally dropped my heart into His hands spiritually, physically, and emotionally. Not too long after, it happened. We began communicating again and were married soon after.

I later learned that God had been working on him too and that he had been asking God to help him make changes that he had been resistant to make on his own. I realized that if I had kept reaching out, putting myself into the situation, maybe pushing things, then it may have worked out differently, and quite possibly, the work that God was doing in his heart may have had a different turnout.

There's something to be said about walking away from a situation, with your dignity intact, and letting God make the way for you, instead of you making a way for yourself.

Which way do you think will last.... yours or God's?

May you seek Him in all you do in life, put everything at His feet and wait for His wisdom.

Thank You

$\mathcal{I}$ want to take a moment to express my heartfelt gratitude for your purchase of my book on Esther. Your support means the world to me, and I am honored that my compilation journey has found a place in your collection.

As a writer, there's nothing more rewarding than knowing my words have reached readers like you. I have poured my heart and soul into the creation this book, and it brings me great joy to think that it will now be a part of your literary journey.

I sincerely hope that its pages bring you moments of inspiration, reflection, and joy. May it deepen and strengthen your walk with the Lord and provide you with the lasting transformation you desire.

Thank you again for choosing to embark on this literary adventure with me. Your support fuels my passion to share more of my journey to help people live freely and THRIVE in every area of life.

I am truly blessed to have you as a reader! If there is anything specific you enjoyed or would like to share about your reading experience, it would be an honor to hear from you.

Warmest regards!

Notes

Notes

Notes

Notes

Notes

Notes

Notes

Notes

Notes

Notes

232

Ann Marie Thrives

Ann Marie is a Skin Care and Self-Care Enthusiast, Certified Human Behavioral Specialist, Coach, Speaker and Author.

For over 40 years she has been empowering women and entrepreneurs towards confidence, well-being, and purpose by helping them heal and become whole from the "inside out." She believes that providing understanding of who we were created to be deep within brings courage and strength to accomplish our life's purpose.

Having suffered spinal and traumatic brain injuries, one of her life's quests was to learn how our brain function affects our bodies and our lives. Despite the struggles, living without pain was a priority, and she has found ways to engage in life and live abundantly.

My journey of self-awareness fostered my wholeness and well-being. The implementation of this knowledge helps me individually and as an entrepreneur.

My desire is to share what I have learned with others and help them to gain confidence, competence and wholeness in their minds and bodies to THRIVE, not survive in every extension of life."

https://linktr.ee/wethriveatlife